Andrew Robinson is the author of some twenty books, including *Satyajit Ray: The Inner Eye* and *Satyajit Ray: A Vision of Cinema* (both I.B.Tauris), and is the editor of three screenplays by Ray. www.andrew-robinson.org

'Satyajit Ray has worked with humility and complete dedication; he has gone down on his knees in the dust. And his picture has the quality of intimate, unforgettable experience.'

—Lindsay Anderson on *Pather Panchali*, 1956

'Though he's very young still, he's the Father of Indian Cinema.'

—Jean Renoir on Ray, 1967

'Not to have seen the cinema of Ray means existing in the world without seeing the sun or the moon.'

—Akira Kurosawa, 1975

'Ray's magic, the simple poetry of his images and their emotional impact, will always stay with me.'

—Martin Scorsese, 1991

The Apu Trilogy

Satyajit Ray and the Making of an Epic

Andrew Robinson

I.B. TAURIS
LONDON · NEW YORK

Published in 2011 by I.B.Tauris & Co Ltd
6 Salem Road, London W2 4BU
175 Fifth Avenue, New York NY 10010
www.ibtauris.com

Distributed in the United States and Canada Exclusively by Palgrave Macmillan
175 Fifth Avenue, New York NY 10010

ISBN 978 1 84885 515 1 (HB)
ISBN 978 1 84885 516 8 (PB)

A full CIP record for this book is available from the British Library
A full CIP record is available from the Library of Congress

Library of Congress Catalog Card Number: available

Printed and bound in Great Britain by
TJ International Ltd, Padstow, Cornwall

Contents

Illustrations

Acknowledgements

Vivid memories of Manikda during the 1980s and my evergreen appreciation of his films were the inspiration for this work – my fourth, and final, book on Satyajit Ray. I hope that it helps to bring a new audience not only to his most famous films, the Apu Trilogy, but also to the rest of his extraordinarily varied output.

I would like to thank Oliver Craske, Nemai Ghosh, Indrani Majumdar, Dilip K. Roy and Chandak Sengoopta for their help over several years, and especially Ujjal Chakraborty, who gave me some invaluable information about the novel *Pather Panchali*, and Marc Riboud, who provided some classic photographs of Ray taken during the making of the Apu Trilogy. The illustrations by Ray are reproduced by agreement with the Satyajit Ray Society.

Philippa Brewster at I.B.Tauris was a supportive editor. Jayne Ansell and Rohini Krishnan took great care in the production of the book.

Satyajit Ray on location in Calcutta, 1956, while shooting *Aparajito*, with cameraman Subrata Mitra

1

Self-taught Film-maker:
Satyajit Ray's Formative Years

'I never imagined that I would become a film director, in command of situations, actually guiding people to do things this way or that,' Satyajit Ray said in the mid-1980s, three decades after making his first film *Pather Panchali*, the beginning of the Apu Trilogy. 'No, I was very reticent and shy as a schoolboy and I think it persisted through college. Even the fact of having to accept a prize gave me goose-pimples. But from the time of *Pather Panchali* I realised that I had it in me to take control of situations and exert my personality over other people and so on – then it became a fairly quick process. Film after film, I got more and more confident.'

Ray was born, an only child, in Calcutta on 2 May 1921, into a distinguished though not wealthy Bengali family notable for its love of music, literature, art and scholarship. His grandfather, Upendrakisore Ray, who died before Satyajit was born, was a pioneer of half-tone printing, a musician and composer of songs and hymns, and a writer and illustrator of classic children's literature. His father, Sukumar Ray, was a writer and illustrator of nonsense literature, the equal of Lewis Carroll and Edward Lear. Both men were also universally considered to be the epitome of courtesy, artists in their lives as much as in their works.

They regarded themselves as Brahmos, that is, Christian-influenced Hindus who rejected caste (Brahminism), idolatry and the Hindu festivals, though not the teachings of the original Hindu scriptures, the *Vedas* and the *Upanishads*. Although Satyajit would regard the social reforming side of Brahmoism as generally admirable, he was not attracted to its theology (or to any theology, for that matter). He said: 'As material for a film' – for example, his film about nineteenth-century Hindu orthodoxy, *The Goddess/Devi* – 'I feel Hinduism is much more interesting than Brahmoism. As a child I found Hinduism much more exciting than Brahmoism, and Christianity too. When I think of Brahmoism I think of solemn sermons mainly. I don't think of being free from the shackles of orthodoxy.' (Parts of the Ray family remained relatively orthodox Hindus, which did not prevent the maintenance of very friendly relations with their Brahmo relatives.)

Of his grandfather Upendrakisore, one of whose stories Ray adapted to make the musical *The Adventures of Goopy and Bagha/ Goopy Gyne Bagha Byne* (by far his most popular film in Bengal), he wrote:

> My grandfather was a rare combination of East and West. He played the *pakhwaj* [drum] as well as the violin, wrote devotional songs while carrying out research on printing methods, viewed the stars through a telescope from his own roof, wrote old legends and folk-tales anew for children in his inimitably lucid and graceful style and illustrated them in oils, water-colours and pen-and-ink, using truly European techniques. His skill and versatility as an illustrator remain unmatched by any Indian.

Of his father, who was the subject of a documentary film, *Sukumar Ray*, made by Satyajit for his father's birth centenary in 1987, he remarked: 'As far as my father's writing and drawing goes, nearly all his best work belongs to his last two and a half years' – after, that is, his father contracted kala-azar, the disease that eventually killed him in 1923 at the age of only 35.

Satyajit was less than two and a half years old then. He retained only one memory of his father. It belonged to the courtyard of a house on the banks of the Ganges outside Calcutta, where the family had gone for the sake of Sukumar's health. His father was sitting indoors by the window painting. He suddenly called out 'Ship coming!' Satyajit remembered running into the courtyard and seeing a steamer pass by with a loud hoot. As a sort of private tribute to this memory, the painting Sukumar was then at work on appears in Ray's documentary.

He had many memories, however, of the house in north Calcutta where he lived with his father's extended family until the age of five or six. It was designed and built by his grandfather as a house-cum-printing-press. Here was printed, apart from Upendrakisore's and Sukumar's books (and other books written by the family), the monthly children's magazine *Sandesh* (a title meaning both 'news' and a kind of milk sweet famous in Bengal), which was founded by Upendrakisore in 1913, edited by Sukumar after grandfather Ray's death and revived, much later, in the 1960s, by Satyajit and other family members.

From very early on he was fascinated, for instance, by the whole paraphernalia of printing, as is clear from the printing press at the centre of Ray's film *Charulata*. Manik (meaning 'jewel') – as the small Satyajit was known in the family – became a frequent visitor to the first floor. When he entered, the compositors, sitting side by side in front of their multi-sectioned typecases, would glance up at him and smile. He would make his way past them to the back of the room, to the block-making section with its enormous imported process camera and its distinctive smells. 'Even today,' wrote Ray in his memoir of his childhood published in *Sandesh* in 1981, 'if I catch a whiff of turpentine, a picture of U. Ray and Sons' block-making department floats before my eyes.' The main operator of the camera, Ramdohin, was his friend. He had had no formal education; Upendrakisore had trained him from scratch and he was like one of the family. Presenting Ramdohin with a piece of paper with some squiggles on it, Manik would announce: 'This is for *Sandesh*.' Ramdohin would solemnly wag his head in agreement, 'Of course, Khoka Babu [Little Master], of course,' and would lift the boy up to show him the upside-down image of his drawing on the screen of the camera. But somehow the drawing would never appear in *Sandesh*.

In early 1927, however, the firm had to be liquidated, because there was no one in the family able to manage it competently. The joint family had no option but to leave the house and split up. Manik and his widowed mother were fortunate to be taken in by one of her brothers, who lived in an up-and-coming part of south Calcutta. Satyajit would live in this uncle's various houses for the rest of his childhood and youth until the age of 27, when he acquired sufficient financial independence to move out. While he was growing up he would never have much money. He did not miss it, though; and in adult life he would simply maintain the relatively spartan habits of his early years. In fact, he felt himself to be rich and seemed surprised if one queried this. 'I mean I have no money worries as such,' he said, 'thanks to my writing' – he meant his dozens of best-selling stories and young people's novels starring his detective Felu Mitter, two of which he filmed – 'not from films really. I'm certainly not as rich as Bombay actors – by no means; but I'm comfortable, I can buy the books and records I want.'

Although the move was a drastic change, Manik did not feel it as a wrench. 'Adults treat all children in such a situation as "poor little creatures", but that is not how children see themselves', he commented in his memoir, articulating his fundamental attitude as perhaps the most natural director of children in cinema, beginning with the boy Apu and his sister Durga in *Pather Panchali*.

Nevertheless, whether he thought of it or not as a child, he was now thrown back on his own resources. He had been taken from a world of writers, artists and musicians, where West mixed freely and fruitfully with East, science with arts, into a typically middle-class milieu of barristers and insurance brokers, with the exception of his mother, an aunt about to become a famous singer of Tagore songs and, a little later, a 'cousin' Bijoya, Satyajit's future wife, who was musical and interested in acting. There were no children of Satyajit's age in the new house. Though he often saw two other girl cousins, Ruby and Nini (Nalini Das, who would later edit *Sandesh* with him), they were somewhat older and he seldom talked to them about himself. Yet in later life Ray did not think of his childhood as lonely: 'Loneliness and being alone – bereft of boys and girls of your own age as friends – is not the same thing. I wasn't envious of little boys with lots of sisters and brothers. I felt I was all right and I had a lot to do, I could keep myself busy doing various things, small things – reading, looking at books and looking at pictures, all sorts of things including sketching. I used to draw a lot as a child.'

As with many only children, he was also a close observer of his elders and noticed that his uncles and their friends in their twenties and thirties did not always behave as if they *were* elders; they had a noisy passion for games like ludo, for instance. The adult Ray said that he must have been 'imbibing' a great deal about people at this time without being aware of it. Certainly, the two decades he spent with his maternal uncles gave him an invaluable grounding in the mores of the Bengali middle class, both as characters for films and as a cinema audience.

Like the lonely wife Charu, wandering round her house in the first seven minutes of *Charulata*, Satyajit was highly sensitive as a child to sounds and lighting. Half a century later, he could remember various vanished street cries and the fact that in those days you could spot the make of a car, such as a Ford, Humber, Oldsmobile, Opal Citroen or La Salle (with its 'boa horn'), from inside the house by the sound of its horn.

Small holes in the fabric of the house taught Satyajit some basic principles of light. At noon in summer rays of bright sunlight shone through a chink in the shutters of the bedroom.

Satyajit would lie there alone watching the 'free bioscope' created on a wall: a large inverted image of the traffic outside. He could clearly make out cars, rickshaws, bicycles, pedestrians and other passing things.

Stereoscopes and magic lanterns were popular toys in Bengali homes of the period. The magic lantern was a box with a tube at the front containing the lens, a chimney at the top and a handle at the right-hand side. The film ran on two reels with a kerosene lamp for light source. 'Who knows?' wrote Satyajit in his memoir. 'Perhaps this was the beginning of my addiction to film?'

Visits to the cinema began while he was still at his grandfather's house and continued when he moved to his uncle's house. Until he was about fifteen, when Satyajit took control of his cinema outings, they were comparatively infrequent and each film would be followed by 'weeks of musing on its wonders'. Although his uncles enjoyed going, they did not altogether approve of the cinema and for many years they restricted Manik to certain foreign films and ruled out Bengali productions as being excessively passionate for the young mind. This suited him well enough, as he had disliked the only Bengali film he saw as a boy. He went to it by accident: an uncle had taken him to see the first Johnny Weismuller *Tarzan* film, but the tickets had all been sold. He saw the dismay on Manik's face and so took him down the road to a Bengali cinema. The film was *Kal Parinay* (The Doomed Marriage) – 'an early example of Indian soft porn', according to Ray, who remembered the hero and the heroine – 'or was it the Vamp?' – newly married and lying in bed, and a close-up showing the woman's leg rubbing the man's. 'I was only nine then, but old enough to realise that I had strayed into forbidden territory.' His uncle made repeated whispered efforts to take him home, but Manik, already precociously dedicated to the cinema, turned a deaf ear. It was not that he was enjoying the film, simply that he was determined to get to the end.

In Calcutta those were the days of Silents, Partial Talkies and One Hundred Per Cent Talkies and, at the grandest cinema in town, a Wurlitzer played by a man called Byron Hopper. The choice of foreign films was quite impressive. Much later, out of curiosity, Ray decided to check the files of the Calcutta *Statesman* for a certain date in 1927 and found six films playing: *Moana* (by Robert Flaherty), *Variety* (a German production by E. A. Dupont), *The Gold Rush* (by Charlie Chaplin), *Underworld* (by Josef von Sternberg), *The Freshman* (with Harold Lloyd) and *The Black Pirate* (with Douglas Fairbanks).

Chaplin, Buster Keaton and Harold Lloyd made a tremendous and lasting impression on Satyajit. So did *The Thief of Baghdad* and *Uncle Tom's Cabin*. Other memories of Hollywood films seen in the 1920s included:

> Lillian Gish, in *Way Down East*, stepping precariously from one floating chunk of ice to another while fiendish blood-hounds nosed along her trail; John Gilbert, as the Count of Monte Cristo, delirious at the sight of gold in a treasure chest; Lon Chaney, as the Hunchback, clutching with dead hands the bell ropes of Notre Dame, and – perhaps the most exciting memory of all – the chariot race in *Ben Hur*, undimmed by a later and more resplendent version, for the simple reason that the new Messala is no match for the old and dearly hated one of Francis X. Bushman.

Stories of romance and passion, even of the foreign variety, remained generally out of bounds, but when he was about eleven Satyajit did get to see several of Ernst Lubitsch's films: *Love Parade*, *The Smiling Lieutenant*, *One Hour with You*, *Trouble in Paradise* – 'a forbidden world, only half-understood, but observed with a tingling curiosity', he later wrote. *Trouble in Paradise* particularly stuck in his mind, showing that Lubitsch's sophisticated wit appealed to Satyajit even then, though revealingly the scene as he remembers it is wordless – like many high points in the Apu Trilogy: 'It opened with a moonlit shot of the romantic Grand Canal in Venice. The inevitable gondola appeared, glided up the glistening water, and, as it moved closer, turned out to be filled with garbage. The fat gondolier pulled up the boat in front of the villa, collected some more garbage and, at the point of rowing off, burst into an aria by Verdi.'

One kind of film permissible to him as a boy that did *not* appeal, either to Manik or to his family, was the British film. Technical superiority notwithstanding, it was marred by the same faults that Ray would ridicule in the typical Bengali cinema of the thirties (and after, he continued to think): stagey settings, theatrical dialogue, affected situations and acting. 'We laughed at Jack Hulbert not mainly because we were tickled, but because we did not want our British neighbours in the theatre to think that we had no sense of humour', he wrote – and this was about as close as he came to the British in Calcutta until he took a job in his early twenties.

As the 1930s wore on, Satyajit saw films more and more frequently, including some Bengali ones. He began to keep a notebook with his own star ratings and learnt to distinguish the finish of the different Hollywood studios. He even wrote a fan letter to Deanna Durbin (and received a very polite reply). But at no point did he consider that he might direct films himself. This idea did not strike him until his late twenties, well after he had left college, although an astrologer to whom his mother insisted on taking him when he was 22 had predicted that he would become internationally famous 'through the use of light'. (Ray forgot all about this prediction until after he had finished *Pather Panchali* in 1955, when his mother reminded him. He had no belief in astrology and always refused requests from palmists to supply an imprint of his hand.)

He also read a lot in these early years, but as with films he was mainly interested in books in English, not in Bengali – he read little of Bengal's greatest writer Rabindranath Tagore until much later, for instance – apart from the ancient stories and folk tales which as a young child he enjoyed hearing told in the Bengali versions of his grandfather and one or two other writers. (He recalled making one of his uncles read him at least four times a particular grisly episode of the *Mahabbharata* in Upendrakisore Ray's retelling, involving severed and exploding heads.) His favourite reading was the *Book of Knowledge*, ten copiously illustrated, self-confidently imperial volumes, and later, the *Romance of Famous Lives*, which his mother bought him; there he first encountered Ludwig van Beethoven and developed an adolescent taste for western painting from the Renaissance up to the beginning of Impressionism. He also liked comics and detective stories, the *Boy's Own Paper* (in which he won a prize for a photograph of Kashmir when he was fifteen), Sherlock Holmes stories and P. G. Wodehouse; and thus he came to believe that London was 'perpetually shrouded in impenetrable fog' and that most homes in England had butlers. Throughout his youth, and to a great extent in later life too, his taste in English fiction was light, rather than classic.

And he developed yet another interest in the arts, one that was distinctly unusual for a Bengali: western classical music. It came upon him, Ray wrote later, 'at an age when the Bengali youth almost inevitably writes poetry' and fast became an obsession. He already owned a hand-cranked Pigmyphone which had been given to him when he was about five by a relative through marriage, the owner of one of the best record shops in Calcutta. The song 'Tipperary' (which appears incongruously in *Pather Panchali*) and 'The Blue Danube' were two of the earliest pieces of music he played on it. When he was about thirteen he began listening to some other records, mainly by Beethoven, that happened to be in the house. His response, perhaps partly because he had been primed by his earlier reading, was one of immense excitement. Here was music that was completely new, totally unlike his grandfather's hymns and Tagore's songs that surrounded him and the Indian instrumental music he also listened to, if without much enthusiasm. With what little money he had, he started hunting for bargains in Calcutta's music shops and attending concerts of the Calcutta Symphony Orchestra, and he joined a gramophone club whose members were almost all

Europeans and Parsees. The number of Bengalis seriously interested in western classical music in Calcutta at this time could be counted on the fingers of two hands – even Tagore was not (though his favourite niece was).

School, which he attended from the age of nine to fifteen, meant comparatively little to Satyajit, though he was never unhappy or unpopular there. And the same was true of his college education at the best institution in Calcutta, Presidency College. As he put it in a lecture, 'My life, my work', given in 1982, when he had turned 60: 'Erudition is something which I singularly lack. As a student, I was only a little better than average, and in all honesty, I cannot say that what I learnt in school and college has stood me in good stead in the years that followed. ... My best and keenest memories of college consist largely of the quirks and idiosyncrasies of certain professors' – as is obvious from Ray's quizzical portrayal of Apu's college professors in *Aparajito*, the second film of the Apu Trilogy.

It was his time at Shantiniketan, Tagore's university in a poor rural district about a hundred miles from Calcutta, where Satyajit was a student of fine arts from 1940 to 1942, which was the part of his formal education that would have a genuine influence on the future course of his life. Without his Shantiniketan experience, *Pather Panchali* would not have been possible, he later realised. No one could explain this better than Ray himself, in his Calcutta lecture:

> My relationship with Shantiniketan was an ambivalent one. As one born and bred in Calcutta, I loved to mingle with the crowd in Chowringhee [the city's most famous thoroughfare], to hunt for bargains in the teeming profusion of second-hand books on the pavements of College Street, to explore the grimy depths of the Chor Bazaar for symphonies at throwaway prices, to relax in the coolness of a cinema, and lose myself in the make-believe world of Hollywood. All this I missed in Shantiniketan, which was a world apart. It was

a world of vast open spaces, vaulted over with a dustless sky, that on a clear night showed the constellations as no city sky could ever do. The same sky, on a clear day, could summon up in moments an awesome invasion of billowing darkness that seemed to engulf the entire universe. And there was the Khoyai [a ravine], rimmed with the serried ranks of *tal* trees, and the [river] Kopai, snaking its way through its rough-hewn undulations. If Shantiniketan did nothing else, it induced contemplation, and a sense of wonder, in the most prosaic and earthbound of minds.

In the two and a half years, I had time to think, and time to realise that, almost without my being aware of it, the place had opened windows for me. More than anything else, it had brought me an awareness of our tradition, which I knew would serve as a foundation for any branch of art that I wished to pursue.

Ironically, Ray's training as a painter in Shantiniketan and its surrounding villages – along with his first-hand, awed confrontation with the wonders of Indian art on a tour of the famous sites (Ajanta, Ellora, Elephanta, Sanchi, Khajuraho, among others) by third-class train in 1941–42 – convinced him that he did not have it in him to be a painter. He admired several of his teachers, especially the artists Binode Bihari Mukherjee and Nandalal Bose, but he decided to leave Shantiniketan without completing the five-year fine arts course. A few months later, in April 1943, he took a job as a commercial artist in Calcutta, with a British-owned advertising agency, D. J. Keymer. He worked as a junior visualiser, having been recommended by someone the Ray family knew to Keymer's assistant manager D. K. Gupta: a man who, as the founder of a new publishing house, was to play a crucial part in Ray's life over the next decade or so. 'I see, you're Sukumar Ray's son. Tell me about the books your father wrote,' were Gupta's first words at the job interview. Within a few years, Ray became the agency's art director.

Although Keymer's was considered more informal than, say, the agency J. Walter Thompson – because it employed fewer British sahibs – it had its share of racial tensions, naturally exacerbated by the charged political atmosphere of the 1940s during the run-up to Indian Independence in 1947. The position of art director, for instance, had to be shared with an Englishman, 'a nice fellow but a shockingly bad artist', wrote Satyajit in 1948 to an English friend in London. 'But he has to be there, being an Englishman, and I have to be there, as part of the Post-Independence Diplomatic Managerial Policy. Of course he gets three times as much as I do.' The managers were all British in the years Ray worked there, a succession of Englishmen and Scotsmen. He liked most of them and did not allow nationalist emotions to cloud his feelings towards them; two or three became friends. They, for their part, treated him with respect and generosity, such was the high standard of design he maintained, calling him Maneck Roy to avoid the tricky 'Satyajit'. One of the managers, J. B. R. Nicholson, probably spoke for them all when he said: 'Ray was a man of real integrity. He had no *chalaki* [trickiness] in him.'

This is not to say that Satyajit ever relished the work or the life of an advertising office, useful background though it was for such films as *The Big City/Mahanagar, Days and Nights in the Forest/Aranyer Din Ratri* and, especially, *Company Limited/ Seemabaddha*. A laconic note in English in his shooting notebook for this last film seems to do duty for his general feelings towards advertising: 'the usual comments are bandied about' – to describe a scene when the lights go up after the screening of a typical 'ad film' and the assembled account executives attempt smart backchat. His usual reaction to this behaviour at Keymer's was an aloof silence. He concentrated his attention on the purely artistic aspects of the job. 'If you had really thought about what you were doing,' he said years later, 'you would have found it a dismaying thought. Partly because the clients were generally so stupid. You'd produce an artwork which was admirable, you'd know it was good, and they'd come out with little criticisms that were so stupid that you'd really want to give up immediately.'

Ray's contribution to the development of advertising imagery in India was certainly distinctive, but hard to define. Like all the best graphic designers, he combined visual flair with a feel for the meaning of words and their nuances. Sometimes this meant changing a headline to fit a layout. According to one colleague, 'He interpreted the words in such a way that he often gave them a new depth of meaning.' He brought to his work a fascination with typography, both Bengali and English, which he shared with his father and grandfather and which would in due course surface in his film credit sequences and film posters for the Apu Trilogy. He also introduced into advertising more calligraphic elements than before (and created the fully calligraphic wedding invitation), as well as genuinely Indian elements: everyday details and motifs from past and present, emphatically not the limp, prettified borrowings from mythology he strongly disliked in what was then considered Oriental Art.

But it was design of a more lasting, less mercenary kind that occupied Ray's best energies during the Keymer's years. Around the end of 1943, the assistant manager D. K. Gupta started Signet Press, a publisher in both Bengali and English, and asked Satyajit to design the books. Ray was given a completely free hand in a publishing field that was as good as virgin.

He began illustrating books too. His first illustrations, created in 1944–45, were some woodcuts of simple vitality for an abridgement for children of Bibhutibhusan Banerji's 1920s novel *Pather Panchali*. Some of these scenes, such as the children Apu and Durga huddling together during the storm, later found their way onto celluloid. At Gupta's suggestion, he read the unabridged novel. 'The book filled me with admiration. It was plainly a masterpiece and a sort of encyclopaedia of life in rural Bengal', Ray recalled in his autobiography *My Years with Apu*. 'It dealt with a Brahmin family, an indigent priest, his wife, his two children and his aged cousin, struggling to make both ends meet. The amazingly lifelike portrayals, not just of the family but of a host of other characters, the vivid details of daily existence, the warmth, the humanism, the lyricism, made the book a classic of its kind.' Gupta, a keen film fan, intrigued Satyajit by telling him that the main story of *Pather Panchali* would make a very good film. Thus the earliest glimmering of Ray's film dates from 1944.

Fruitful though all this was, and financially rewarding too, Ray's relationship with Gupta suffered from the kind of strain inevitable when a publisher tries to combine quality with commercial viability. They clashed, for example, over some books very close to Satyajit's heart, those by his father, Sukumar Ray. Signet Press republished these but changed the formats and had them re-illustrated, against the wishes of Satyajit and his mother. On balance though, Ray felt grateful to Gupta for a unique opportunity at a time when it could not have been more welcome. Signet enabled him to experiment with a wide range of styles and techniques of drawing, painting and typography and gave him a growing familiarity with fiction in Bengali to offset his earlier predilection for English literature. By his mid-thirties, Ray had acquired a clear sense of the strengths and weaknesses of Bengali literature from both a literary and a cinematic point of view.

A novel which appeared around this time and greatly impressed him was Bibhutibhusan Banerji's *Asani Sanket*. In 1972, Ray filmed it with restrained pathos as *Distant Thunder*. Through the eyes of a village Brahmin priest and his wife, it shows the beginnings of the famine of 1943–44 that killed at least three and a half million Bengalis. When the famine reached Calcutta from the villages, in August 1943, Ray had been at Keymer's for nearly six months. The causes of the famine, though undoubtedly connected with the Second World War, were complex and did few groups in British-Indian society much credit, but the government reaction, then and in the months to come, was a matter for shame. Given the extent of official apathy, it is perhaps not surprising that Ray, along with most people he knew, did nothing to help the victims, but the famine left him with a lasting sense of shame. 'One gets used to everything ultimately,' he said four decades later, after considerable pondering – including stepping over corpses lying in the street outside his house and the 'refrain' of the victims' cries for *phyan*, the water usually thrown out once rice has been boiled. The reason that he gave for his general indifference was honest, if a bit shocking: he felt that at this time he was 'getting established in life. New fields were opening before me, and there was my *intense* absorption into western music which was then at its height. So if one said I was a little callous about the famine, one wouldn't be far wrong; because one just got used to it, and there was nobody doing anything about it. It was too vast a problem for anyone to tackle.' Nonetheless, the grim exposure prepared Ray's mind to depict poverty sympathetically in *Pather Panchali*.

The period 1943–47 was, in fact, a most extraordinary one in the history of the second city of the British empire, with the 1947 partition of India following hard on the aftermath of the famine. Trains from East Bengal (as it became East Pakistan) unloaded their contents on the railway platforms of Calcutta where they remained, whole families taking up just four to six square feet of space, including babies born on the spot. The immediate impact of the world war was negligible by comparison. Although Calcutta was bombed by the Japanese and hundreds of thousands left the city, damage was slight. It was the influx of American GIs and other Allied servicemen that changed things and gave a kick to the city's cultural life. For the first time in Calcutta it was normal to read a review of a Hollywood movie *after* seeing it, probably in a wafer-thin copy of *Time* magazine. Because of the war, Ray was able to see Hollywood films that had not been released even in London.

Music too was excellent, including jazz, which Satyajit enjoyed for a while. Apart from performances of Indian music, especially by the prodigy Ravi Shankar, which Ray had begun to attend, there were concerts by visiting western musicians such as Isaac Stern. On the BBC World Service he listened to Narayana

Menon in London playing J. S. Bach on the *vina*, and on Berlin radio to some good classical music broadcast along with Hitler's speeches. And in Bombay, where he had relatives and his 'cousin' Bijoya was living for a while, he discovered a source of miniature scores of western classical music and began buying them and reading them in bed. He taught himself western musical notation partly by comparing the score with his phenomenal musical memory, which could retain a symphony once he had heard it three times or so. At this time, of course, all the available recordings were on 78 rpm records and he discovered that 'although the top line [of the score] could be heard clearly enough, a great many details which one could *see* on the page were virtually inaudible in the recording.'

Until early 1948, Satyajit and his mother continued to live in his uncle's house. He had been looking for a flat for some time – not an easy task in wartime, as he mentioned in a 1945 letter to one of his friends from Shantiniketan days, the musical Alex Aronson: 'I propose to have a room of my own which should be a library-cum-studio-cum-concert-room affair.' The apartment he eventually found was by no means all he had hoped: 'not nearly as much comfort as I used to have in my uncle's house', he lamented in a letter to another European friend a month or so after moving. 'The noise in the neighbourhood is terrific. Radios, gramophones, yelling babies and what not. The first few days were really nerve racking. But I'm getting used to it slowly. I can play the gramophone only after things have quietened down around half past ten or eleven at night.' Nevertheless, the experience proved useful later when he dramatised the crowded, noisy, lower middle-class flat in *The Big City*.

He was writing to the man who had become his first British friend, Norman Clare. Music and war had brought them together while Clare was in the Royal Air Force in Calcutta from late 1944 until early 1946; for three months at the end of 1945, Clare stayed in the house of Satyajit's uncle, just as, five years later, Satyajit and his wife would stay in the house of Clare's mother on their first visit to London in 1950. Each day, Clare remembered, when Satyajit returned home from Keymer's, he would immediately change out of western clothes into a *dhoti* or pyjama. Then he and Norman would chat, go and see a film, listen to music – Wilhelm Furtwängler being their favourite conductor – or play chess. 'There was a long time when I did nothing but play chess in the evening,' recalled Ray. After Clare left Calcutta he had no partner, so he took up solitaire chess; the habit wore off as he became engrossed in film-making but much later resurfaced in the form of *The Chess Players/Shatranj ke Khilari*.

Clare remembered Satyajit as a gregarious person, whatever his aloofness at the office. Throughout his life Ray was usually open with people when he was interested in what they were saying or doing; it was only otherwise that he would tend to withdraw into himself and give the 'aristocratic', even arrogant, impression for which he would often be criticised in later life. For many years from the mid-1940s he used to meet a group of friends at a coffee house near Keymer's for an *adda*, a word that embraces extended gossip on every conceivable subject (Ray once translated it as 'talkathon'). 'Do not look down upon the *addas* in the Calcutta tea and coffee shops,' an energetic Calcutta professor used to warn those who criticised Bengalis for being all talk and no action. 'They are unrecognised universities where heads clash and ideas emerge' – which was certainly true of Satyajit's *adda* during the making of *Pather Panchali* in the early 1950s. In his *addas* in the coffee house he taught his friends quite a bit, learnt something himself (especially about how to deal with people), and had a lot of fun, which included sharpening his English on the London *Times* crossword then published on the back page of the Calcutta *Statesman*. The coffee house brought out a chatty, relaxed side of Ray that non-Bengalis seldom saw, especially after old-style *addas* had rather disappeared with the post-war pressures of Calcutta life. Four decades on, the sad decline of the *adda* would form a key topic of conversation in Ray's last film, *The Stranger/Agantuk*.

Some of the members of the coffee-house group would play a role in Ray's film career, notably Bansi Chandragupta, a Kashmiri who was then a dissatisfied art director in Bengali cinema and who soon became Ray's long-time art director. Cinema was endlessly discussed, particularly after Satyajit and another member of the group, Chidananda Das Gupta, had founded the Calcutta Film Society in late 1947. 'I am taking the cinema more and more seriously', Ray wrote to Clare in May 1948. He went regularly to the cinema alone, but also took along his friends after work on Saturdays, paying for them himself. At the time he took up his advertising job in 1943 he had already read two theoretical books on film-making (by Rudolf Arnheim and Raymond Spottiswoode) while studying at Shantiniketan, and had graduated from an admiration for stars and studios to a focus on directors. Now he began to make 'hieroglyphic notes' in the dark on their various cutting methods, particularly those of the Americans. Through his contacts with American serviceman, and otherwise, he saw recent Hollywood films by Frank Capra, John Ford, John Huston, Lewis Milestone, Billy Wilder and William Wyler. He also saw a film made by Jean Renoir while he was in Hollywood, *The Southerner*, which he greatly liked. 'This was the film that first brought home to me that characters in a film needn't be black or white, but could also be grey', he later wrote. 'It also taught me the importance of shooting in and around locations rather than artificial studio sets meant to represent exteriors.'

Russian films too were available: Mark Donskoi's *The Childhood of Gorky*, Vsevolod Pudovkin's *Storm over Asia*, Sergei Eisenstein's *Alexander Nevsky* and *Ivan the Terrible Part 1*, and others. *Ivan* made a tremendous impression, though not entirely for its filmic qualities: 'The Gothic gloom of the film, [Nikolai] Cherkasov's grand gestures, and the music of [Sergei] Prokofiev stayed with me all the day and well into the night, until I fell asleep and found them back in a grotesque dream, in the middle of which I woke up gasping for breath. It turned out that a *pan* [betel-nut preparation] I had bought from a shop next to the cinema had given me quinsy, swelling the inside of my throat to the point where I could hardly breathe.'

Ray came to the conclusion around this time that Eisenstein's films reminded him of Bach and Pudovkin's of Beethoven. Bengali films remained on his menu too. They had somewhat improved with the arrival of the directors Bimal Roy and Nitin Bose (an uncle of Satyajit), but chiefly in the technical sense; their acting, dialogue and settings remained theatrical. One exception, which made a virtue of its theatricality, was the dance fantasy *Kalpana*, the work of the dancer Uday Shankar (Ravi Shankar's elder brother) which Satyajit saw many times during 1948. 'I never knew Indian music and dancing could have such an impact on me', he wrote to Clare. The film also contained some daring cutting. In the darkness of the cinema hall, Ray took a series of still photographs of the shots that most appealed to him.

Around 1946, he began writing film scripts as a hobby. He acquired a copy of René Clair's published script *The Ghost Goes West* and also the 1943 anthology *Twenty Best Film Plays*, compiled by John Gassner and Dudley Nichols. When plans for a Bengali film were announced he would write a scenario for it, in fact, often two scenarios – 'his' way and 'their' way. In all he wrote ten or twelve such scenarios.

The analysis involved in this led to his first published film criticism, 'What is wrong with Indian films?', which appeared in the Calcutta *Statesman* in 1948. Anticipating the 1950s polemics of *Cahiers du Cinéma*, Ray dissected the failure of Indian directors to grasp the nature of the medium and concluded with a resounding manifesto: 'The raw material of cinema is life itself. It is incredible that a country that has inspired so much painting and music and poetry should fail to move the film-maker. He has only to keep his eyes open, and his ears. Let him do so.' Although he did not mention *Pather Panchali* by name, the idea of his filming the novel was now forming in his mind.

The Calcutta Film Society started a bulletin, which Ray designed, using the resources of Keymer's and Signet Press. Actors, directors and other film people visiting Calcutta were invited to speak. Cherkasov and Pudovkin, Renoir and Huston each spoke there at various times. Ray asked Cherkasov how he had managed to get his eyes so wide open in *Ivan*, because looking at him it did not seem possible. Cherkasov replied that Eisenstein had forced him to do it. 'He was slightly critical of the way he was handled by Eisenstein, made to assume postures that were very difficult, "so that at the end of the day I would have muscle pains all over my body".'

Then, during 1948, a member of the coffee-house group, the wealthy Harisadhan Das Gupta (a future documentary film director), bought the film rights to Tagore's novel *The Home and the World* and embarked with Ray on an attempt to turn it into a movie. They were an ill-matched pair, and the whole venture had an air of farce about it, painful though it was for both of them at the time. Satyajit wrote a script and, along with Bansi Chandragupta as art director, they began looking for locations and properties, an actress to play Tagore's heroine Bimala, and a producer. Das Gupta opened an office with a huge table and very comfortable chairs and acquired a company name and a letterhead designed by Ray. Friends gathered round for tea and *adda*. A potential producer appeared. He promised several hundred thousand rupees in backing. 'All we had to do was go to Nepal and collect some gold bars, *then* make the film,' recalled Das Gupta with a wry chuckle. But in the end the project collapsed, because Ray refused to make the changes to his script required by another producer. He felt 'like a pricked balloon' at the time, yet when he re-read the screenplay in the mid-1960s, he decided it was 'the greatest good fortune the film was never made.' He could see 'how pitifully superficial and Hollywoodish' his tyro screenplay was. He ignored it altogether when he eventually came to film *The Home and the World/Ghare Baire* in the early 1980s.

The following year, 1949, both Das Gupta and Ray were able to be of considerable assistance to Renoir when he visited Calcutta in search of locations and actors for his Indian film, *The River.* Meeting Renoir changed Ray's life; not in an abrupt manner, which would have been uncharacteristic of Ray's response to people, but because Renoir's attitudes to both life and film-making appealed to him in their wholeness. It is not that Renoir and Ray were all that similar as personalities, rather that Ray recognised in Renoir a real film artist – the first he had come to know personally – and drew strength for his own vision from the knowledge that such a person existed. Renoir openly encouraged Ray to film *Pather Panchali* and requested him not to imitate Hollywood films. 'I think what Hollywood really needs is a good bombing', Renoir told Ray. 'In America, they worry too much about technique, and neglect the human aspect.' In 1983, Ray told an interviewer: 'I think that subconsciously I have been paying tribute to Renoir throughout my film-making career.' A few years later, while receiving the Legion of Honour award from the president of France in Calcutta, Ray told him that he had always considered Renoir to be his 'principal mentor'.

The shooting of *The River* began in Bengal in late 1949 and continued through the first half of 1950. Bansi Chandragupta assisted Renoir's art director Eugene Lourié; Subrata Mitra, soon to be Ray's lighting cameraman, took stills. Ray himself was present as an observer on two or three occasions but was unable to get further involved. There was his job at Keymer's to consider, and the fact that his British boss had offered to send him to London for six months' training. 'Doubtless the management hoped that I would come back a fully fledged advertising man wholly dedicated to the pursuit of selling tea and biscuits', he later remarked.

He had also at last married the girl he had known since the early thirties. Bijoya Das was the youngest grand-daughter of his mother's aunt, which made her a kind of cousin to Satyajit: a fact that inevitably provoked comment in Calcutta. She had kept up her love of music – and even made recordings as a singer in Bengali – and her childhood interest in acting had led to a brief unhappy spell in Hindi films in Bombay; she had also been a teacher and government servant in Calcutta. They married in Bombay in October 1948 with the minimum of fuss, just the signing of a register, but Satyajit's mother and his wife's elder sisters later persuaded them to have a very simple ceremony in Calcutta with a Brahmo flavour.

For many months their plans were uncertain. Satyajit's mother fell very seriously ill. When she recovered, he and his wife had to make sure she would be properly cared for in their absence abroad. Then there was his passionate interest in Renoir's shooting of *The River* to consider. At last, the Rays sailed for Europe in April 1950.

Keymer's London office was near the Strand and Satyajit went there every day by bus from Hampstead, where he and Bijoya were living with the mother of Norman Clare. It turned out to be smaller than the Calcutta office, which amused him. But after he had been there a month or so, an unpleasant incident occurred in which he was provoked into losing control of himself for almost the first and last time in his life. 'It was a face-to-face confrontation,' Ray recalled in the 1980s, 'the sort of thing I generally avoid.' He had overheard his boss, a Mr Ball, claiming credit for a poster Keymer's had done for the *Observer* which was, in fact, Ray's work. Without abusing the man, he made it quite clear that he could not accept him as a boss and walked out. Luckily, he was immediately able to join Benson's, another agency nearby, because it was a part of Keymer's. His British manager wrote from Calcutta expressing his full support.

Ray remained upset about the incident for days. Discussing it with his first biographer Marie Seton some years later, he said, 'I had always thought the English in England were better people than the English who come to India.' Probably out of sensitivity for the embarrassment it might cause his friend Norman, he did not even mention the matter to him, but he did tell Norman's mother about it because she asked; she had noticed a persistent scowl on his face.

Satyajit and Bijoya did a lot of walking in London during their five months there. He was determined to go to as many exhibitions, concerts, plays and, most of all, movies as he could. The two Rays stuck to the city and visited nowhere outside it, not even Oxford and Cambridge, favourite haunts of educated Indians. And he made relatively few friends among the English. Apart from Norman Clare and his immediate family, there was really only Lindsay Anderson, then on the staff of the film magazine *Sequence*, with whom he had earlier exchanged letters from Calcutta concerning an article Satyajit wrote for *Sequence*, 'Renoir in Calcutta'. He and Lindsay saw some films together, including at the occasional film society viewing session lasting ten or twelve hours (where Ray saw Dovzhenko's *Earth*).

Anderson and Ray were friends, but never intimate. 'I always knew Satyajit to be intelligent and sympathetic and I suppose that's fairly rare,' said Anderson in the 1980s. 'I think I knew instinctively there were areas we wouldn't share, but you didn't worry about them.' Although Anderson encouraged Ray from London by letter during the long struggle to make *Pather Panchali* after 1950, Ray never volunteered his thoughts on making the novel into a film while he was staying in London. Anderson was not surprised by this. 'Satyajit is a guarded person; it all goes together with the kind of artist he is after all. He's not someone who would ever make himself easily accessible.'

The chief sticking point between them, then and later, was John Ford's work. Both of them certainly admired it, but where Anderson's admiration bordered on 'deification' (to use Ray's word), Ray's stopped well short of this. He disliked Ford's 'sentimentality', his 'excessive proneness to nostalgia' and 'his readiness to yield to commercial pressures'. But, he said, 'Lindsay was absolutely up in arms and wouldn't come down. Even in letters we fought, we argued about it; he over-praised certain things in *Sequence* and I had my own view about it.' To which Anderson said, 'I responded to Ford probably more deeply than he did, because I would probably respond to the emotional quality in Ford more than he would. But it's not something one can be heavy about.'

Of the hundred or so films that Ray saw while he was in London, the revelations were unquestionably Vittorio de Sica's *Bicycle Thieves*, closely followed by Renoir's *The Rules of the Game*. *Bicycle Thieves* 'gored' him, Ray said. 'I came out of the theatre my mind fully made up. I would become a film-maker', he remarked in 1982 in his lecture 'My life, my work' (though, characteristically, he did not let on about this decision even to Clare). 'The prospect of giving up a safe job didn't daunt me any more. I would make my film exactly as De Sica had made his: working with non-professional actors, using modest resources, and shooting on actual locations. The village which Bibhutibhusan [Banerji] had so lovingly described would be a living backdrop to the film, just as the outskirts of Rome were for De Sica's film.'

In an excited letter to Chandragupta in Calcutta, Ray inadvertently revealed his future guiding principle as a film-maker, rejecting Hollywood films as his model:

> The entire conventional approach (as exemplified by even the best American and British films) is wrong. Because the conventional approach tells you that the best way to tell a story is to leave out all except those elements which are directly related to the story, while the master's work clearly indicates that if your theme is strong and simple, then you can include a hundred little apparently irrelevant details which, instead of obscuring the theme, only help to intensify it by contrast, and in addition create the illusion of actuality better.

In a review of *Bicycle Thieves* he wrote for the Calcutta Film Society's bulletin, in which he largely dismissed the Italian films he had seen in London (including Roberto Rossellini's *Rome, Open City*), Ray seemed virtually to describe *Pather Panchali*:

> Zavattini's [De Sica's script writer] greatest assets are an acute understanding of human beings and an ability to devise the 'chain' type of story that fits perfectly into the 90-minute span of the average commercial cinema. Simplicity of plot allows for intensive treatment, while a whole series of interesting and believable situations and characters sustain interest...
>
> *Bicycle Thieves* is a triumphant rediscovery of the fundamentals of cinema, and De Sica has openly acknowledged his debt to Chaplin. The simple universality of its theme, the effectiveness of its treatment, and the low cost of its production make it the ideal film for the Indian film-maker to study. The present blind worship of technique emphasises the poverty of genuine inspiration among our directors. For a popular medium, the best kind of inspiration should derive from life and have its roots in it. No amount of technical polish can make up for artificiality of theme and dishonesty of treatment. The Indian film-maker must turn to life, to reality. De Sica, and *not* De Mille, should be his ideal.

Ray and his wife left London in September 1950, heading for the galleries and concert halls of the Continent before sailing for home about a month later. They visited Lucerne, attended the music festival at Salzburg and the Biennale in Venice and spent a week in Paris where their money ran very low. In Salzburg they were determined to hear Furtwängler conduct the Vienna Philharmonic in Mozart's *The Magic Flute*, which Ray regarded as 'the most enchanting, the most impudent and the most sublime of Mozart's operas'. But the tickets were all sold. Cheated by an usher, who charged them three times the ticket price and then absconded, they stood for half an hour in an aisle until two German youths gave up their seats to them, saying in English, 'You must be from India.' Perhaps their generosity was an

Ray reading a music score, London, 1950

unacknowledged tribute to Tagore's unique and overwhelming impact in Germany in the 1920s.

From Venice, Ray dropped another line to Chandragupta (who had now finished shooting *The River* with Renoir): 'Venice is a fantastic place – very reminiscent of Benares in some ways, and equally photogenic.' His comment had a curious prescience about it. Seven years later, he would come back to Venice for a different reason: to collect, most unexpectedly to him, the Golden Lion award at the Venice Film Festival for the second part of the Apu Trilogy, *Aparajito*, which opens, immortally, on the ghats of Benares.

On board ship returning to India in October 1950, he at long last started to draft his script for *Pather Panchali*.

2

Apu in Fiction and Film: Adapting the Novels *Pather Panchali* and *Aparajito*

The majority of Satyajit Ray's 30 or so feature films were based – sometimes closely, often loosely – on published short stories, novellas and novels. The Apu Trilogy is no exception. However, for all its strong narrative thread, the trilogy looks so essentially cinematic that its literary origin is often underappreciated or even forgotten. For example, the critic Robin Wood, in his significant study of the Apu Trilogy published in 1972, makes only a single glancing reference to the existence of a literary original and does not once mention its author Bibhutibhusan Banerji*. Yet, Ray himself was always happy to acknowledge his profound debt to Banerji's writings, especially in regard to *Pather Panchali*, in which most of the film's dialogue comes from the novel.

The three films in the trilogy – *Pather Panchali/The Song of the Little Road* (1955), *Aparajito/The Unvanquished* (1956) and *Apur Sansar/The World of Apu* (1959) – are based on two novels by Banerji: *Pather Panchali* and its sequel *Aparajito*. The

---

*Banerji is an anglicised spelling of Bandopadhyay, the more accurate Bengali spelling of the name often used today.

first film is a close adaptation of four-fifths of the novel *Pather Panchali*. The second film is based, less closely, on the final fifth of the novel *Pather Panchali* combined with just over a third of the novel *Aparajito*. The third film – the name of which, *Apur Sansar*, was given by Ray – is loosely based on some key incidents in *Aparajito* selected by him mainly from the middle portion of the novel, modified and extended by his own inventive powers. Indeed, Ray did not have in mind three films when he started *Pather Panchali* in 1950. Only after this film's success at the box-office did he decide to tackle a sequel; and only after a substantial hiatus following the release of *Aparajito*, which lost money at the box-office, was he persuaded by public demand to consider the possibility of finding a third film in Banerji's second novel.

By the time he began writing his script of *Pather Panchali*, the novel had become a popular classic in Bengali, assisted by the publication of the abridged edition with Ray's illustrations in the mid-1940s. But when it first started to appear as a serial in a Calcutta journal in 1928, the publisher imposed a condition that the serial could be discontinued if it proved unpopular with readers; both its style and its author were then unknown. However, the story of Apu and Durga rapidly established itself in the imaginations and hearts of Bengali readers; the novel appeared in book form in late 1929, became a school text in its abridged edition, and has never gone out of print. In a respected survey of Bengali literature by the poet and critic Buddhadeva Bose, written in 1948, *Pather Panchali* is described as 'one of the few completely satisfying Bengali novels. ... For it is a book of great beauty, the beauty of childhood and old age, of furrows and flowers, of distances, and of innocence.' *Aparajito*, by contrast, published in 1932, pleased Bose (and the Bengali public) somewhat less: 'The boy-hero Apu grows up and comes to Calcutta where he is as much lost as his author. Love and death, poverty and suffering are all there, but the magic is gone and the glory departed; instead of being an inhabitant of the universe, Apu now is merely a country cousin.' Although Banerji wrote about 50 published works in all, his first book, *Pather Panchali*, remains by far his best-known work, both in Bengal and abroad, after it was published in English and French in the late 1960s as a direct consequence of the success of Ray's film.

The novel was based, to a great extent, on Banerji's own distressingly impecunious early life. He was born in 1894 in a village north of Calcutta. Like Apu's father, Bibhutibhusan's father was a lowly Brahmin priest, an expositor of Hindu mythology, a story-teller, who also had a good voice for singing traditional songs. His mother was an unremarkable village girl. The family lived in extreme poverty, as a consequence of the father's impracticality. Although it included no daughter like Durga in the novel, Bibhutibhusan had a female cousin, a bit older than him, who fits the character Durga, judging from the diary Banerji kept, which also mentions an old aunt who lived with the family – the model for Indir Thakrun, the ancient dependant relative of *Pather Panchali*. Both the father and the mother died in poverty, and the 'sister' was taken by a crocodile (a not-uncommon fate for village children living beside the rivers of Bengal a century ago, which befalls a child in the prologue to the novel).

Somehow, Banerji managed to matriculate from a local school and obtain a degree at Ripon College in Calcutta, again like his hero Apu. Whilst still at college, he married, but lost his young wife a year later in the great influenza epidemic of 1918. Like Apu (who loses his young wife in childbirth), Bibhutibhusan was devastated by the loss; although he had several subsequent romantic attachments, he did not marry again until his mid-forties and had his only child, a son, when he was in his fifties. Meanwhile he became a teacher, living at first in a squalid bazaar near the railway station of a village outside Calcutta, until moving back to the city around 1924. Yet he never felt settled in the metropolis: Banerji (like Tagore, but unlike Ray) always tended to regard Calcutta as an insular place that alienated him from both nature and humanity, and preferred to travel all over India – a wanderlust also seen in Apu.

'In his novels he showed an astonishing capacity for detailed observation of both nature and human character, combined with great humour and tenderness in describing what his observation discovered', said the writer Nirad C. Chaudhuri, an exacting literary critic and a contemporary in age, who became a close friend of Banerji at this time and helped him to get his novel published in both serial and book form. 'His hard life had not embittered him, nor made him a cynic. His sympathy for ordinary people was unlimited, and he was not repelled even by the squalor in which such people had to live in our society. Somehow, he could always make them rise above their surroundings; I would even say – far above the limitations of their world.' In Banerji's personal life, however, Chaudhuri admitted, 'I saw often that he could be totally indifferent even to those very near him. It may have come from his intensely egocentric nature or from the first sorrow of his life which made him grow a protective callousness.' This callousness is reflected in Apu's

Pather Panchali: Apu

extraordinary indifference to the fate of his infant son, which underlies the second half of *The World of Apu*.

Pather Panchali is a novel with a plethora of characters in it: Ray counted more than 300 of them, of whom 30 appear in his film, such as the comical village schoolmaster and the fat itinerant sweetseller. But the main ones, as in the film, are the growing boy Apu, his elder sister Durga, their mother Sarbajaya and father Harihar Ray, a Brahmin priest, and Harihar's elderly distant relative Indir. There is also an extended prologue about the ancestry of the Ray family, one of whom was a brutal robber who committed murders; the shadow of his deeds is thought to have fallen on succeeding generations, including Harihar. The sad history of Indir Thakrun, who is about 75 when the main story begins, is also described. She is very soon dead, treated with extreme callousness by Sarbajaya, who cannot bear to share with her what meagre food she can scrape together; Durga's affection for the old woman cannot save her. The bulk of the novel is about the small family's struggle to survive in their ancestral home in the village. Durga dies of a fever, and the house decays beyond repair. Eventually Harihar decides to pull up his roots and leave. He, his wife and Apu depart for Benares where their life continues; Ray incorporated this section into *Pather Panchali*'s sequel, *Aparajito*.

His adaptation involved drastic compression, elision and omission of scenes in the novel, as well as occasional additions. Out of a seemingly random sequence of significant and trivial episodes, Ray had to extract a simple theme, while preserving the loitering impression created by the original. 'The script had to retain some of the rambling quality of the novel,' commented Ray, 'because that in itself contained a clue to the feel of authenticity: life in a poor Bengali village does ramble.' Much of the power of the film lies in this calculated enriching of an elemental situation by contrasts: as Durga delights her hungry old 'auntie' with a stolen fruit, her mother Sarbajaya ticks her off for taking it; as Indir Thakrun goes off to die in the forest, Apu and Durga bubble with life; and as Harihar returns to the village, terribly overdue but happy because he is bearing gifts for his wife and children, a despairing Sarbajaya can think only of Durga, the child who has left them forever during her husband's long absence from home in search of employment.

Major changes made to the novel by Ray all have their rationale and do not diminish it. Indir's death, for instance, takes place well into the film (over half-way through) when we have got to know her well, and also out in the open so that the two children stumble across her corpse and appreciate the meaning of Death; in the novel she dies early on at a village shrine in someone's house, and only adults are present. Nor, in the novel, do either of the children ever catch sight of a railway train (probably the most famous scene in the film) until Apu, alone, boards a train after leaving the village – though they do attempt to. Nor is Durga's death the direct consequence of getting drenched in the monsoon; the cause of her fever in the novel is left mysterious. Finally, there is the ending of the film: Ray felt, as have all others who have abridged or translated the novel, that the departure from the village for Benares formed a natural break.

The only valid criticism of Ray's approach might lie in the film's attenuated sense of the village of Nishchindipur as a whole. In the novel we learn more about Harihar's ancestors and Nishchindipur's history and geography; there is, for instance, a ruined indigo factory with a child's gravestone still visible belonging to the son of a long-departed British planter's family. And we thereby gain a deeper feeling of Harihar's roots there, which in turn strengthens our understanding of his reluctance to leave his house after disaster befalls him and his family.

Ray's principal challenge in turning *Pather Panchali* into a film was, ironically enough, to dispel his personal ignorance of village life. Unlike Tagore, and many other Bengali writers such as Banerji, the city-dweller Ray had very little first-hand knowledge of the village apart from what he had seen in the villages around Shantiniketan while sketching and painting as an art student in the early 1940s. He had to invent ways to convey on screen the all-important atmosphere of *Pather Panchali*, which is full of descriptions such as this:

> Durga was a big girl now, and her mother would no longer let her go to parties far from home. She had almost forgotten what *luchis* [thin fried bread] tasted like. Until a little while ago, when the nights were bright with the full moon of September and the path through the bamboo grove was like a thread woven of light and shade, she used to wander all round the village and come back with her sari full of sweets and dried, pressed and toasted rice for the Lakshmi festival. At this time of the year conches were being blown in every house, and all along the path floated the smell of frying *luchis*. She always hoped that somebody in the village would send some as part of the festival offering. Whatever sweets she brought back were made to last for two days and her mother had some too. This year however Sejbou [their shrewish neighbour] had said to her mother, 'It isn't right for a girl of a good family to wander round from house to house collecting sweets as if she were a peasant girl. It doesn't look nice.' So from then on she was not allowed to go.

As Ray beautifully depicted the problem in his 1982 Calcutta lecture,

> You had to find out for yourself how to catch the hushed stillness of dusk in a Bengali village, when the wind drops and turns the ponds into sheets of glass, dappled by the leaves of *saluk* and *sapla*, and the smoke from ovens settles in wispy trails over the landscape, and the plaintive blows on conchshells from homes far and near are joined by the chorus of crickets, which rises as the light falls, until all one sees are the stars in the sky, and the stars that blink and swirl in the thickets.

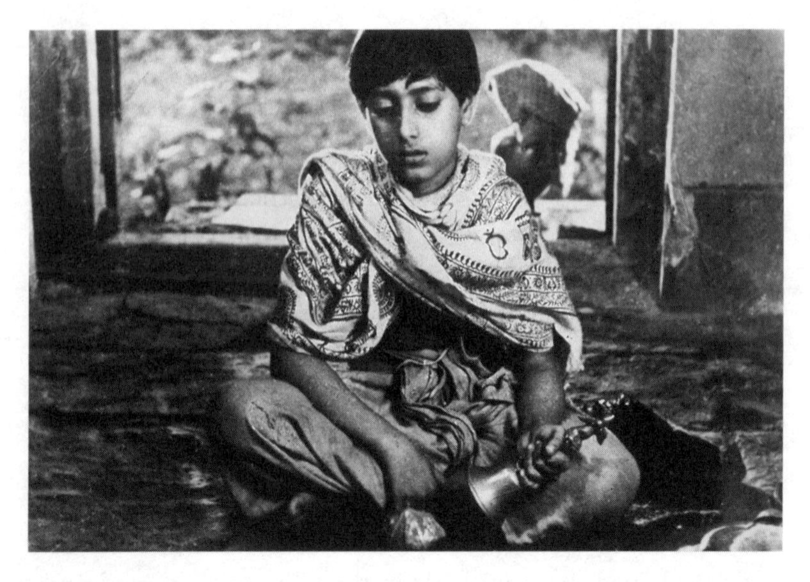

Aparajito: Apu

We shall see how Ray solved some of the problems in practice in the next chapter on the making of the film.

Whilst *Pather Panchali* (in Ray's version) never leaves the village and its environs, *Aparajito* is a film that is constantly on the move as Apu grows up and becomes restless for new experience. It opens in Benares in 1920 with the ten-year-old Apu freely wandering the bathing ghats, narrow lanes and Hindu temples of the sacred city. A welter of new impressions play upon his receptive young mind: the daily rhythm of ablutions in the Ganges at the ghats; the contrasting styles of the various priests who sit there reciting – some earthy, others spiritual like his father; a muscleman swinging a club who offers him a go; pigeons, cows and monkeys everywhere; festival firework displays and sparklers to hold. He also encounters his family's upstairs neighbour Nanda Babu, a sluggardly bachelor who feels obliged to tell the angelic Apu that the liquor bottles in his room are medicine prescribed by his doctor. A little later, as

Harihar lies dying of pneumonia, Nanda Babu will make a pass at Sarbajaya.

Harihar's death leaves his widow with no choice but to take a job. Sarbajaya works as a cook for a rich Bengali Brahmin family in Benares, whilst Apu plucks the grey hairs of the head of the household and does other odd jobs around the house in exchange for a few *paise*. The situation is a dead end for both mother and son, and she knows it. When an older relative of hers, Bhabataran, invites Sarbajaya and Apu to settle in his village in Bengal, she soon accepts and leaves the city.

Apu spends the next five or six years of his life in this new village. His elders expect him to follow tradition and become a priest like his father. But it is the crowd of boys from the local school who really appeal to Apu. He wins over his mother by agreeing to carry out his religious duties too and proves himself a star pupil at school, with a penchant for science. Years of reading and enquiry pass, and we see an older Apu with the beginnings of a moustache standing bashfully before the headmaster again, accepting a scholarship to study science in distant Calcutta. Only his mother stands in the way; her health is beginning to fail and, anyway, she feels Apu should be a priest. They quarrel and she slaps him; then, consumed with remorse, she agrees to let him go and to pay his way in the big city.

The rest of *Aparajito* is a deeply experienced clash between mother and son, and between incompatible beliefs. In Calcutta, studying during the day and earning his keep at night in a printing press, Apu grows distant – mentally as well as physically – from Sarbajaya, whilst she, in the village, as inexorably declines into morbid depression. On a night sparkling with evanescent fireflies, her life leaves her. Apu returns to the village too late. After weeping bitterly, he finds the strength of mind to reject the shade of his father's life and retrace his steps to make a new life in Calcutta. He will definitely not become a priest, though it is not yet clear where his talents will lead him.

The World of Apu: Apu

When the third film, *The World of Apu*, opens, Apu is a graduate without either a job or much desire to get one. He is writing a novel about his struggle to live and hopes to become a writer. Living alone in a dingy garret room above a railway yard in the sprawl of Calcutta, with only his books and his flute for company, he is a figure ripe for romance – something of which he has not an iota of practical experience, as his old college friend Pulu bluntly points out. Pulu has tracked Apu down, determined to drag his friend off to his cousin Aparna's wedding in a village beside a river in East Bengal (now Bangladesh). Over a much-needed decent meal in a restaurant, Apu gives in to Pulu's request, and in the boat on the way to the village, Pulu reads his manuscript and excitedly proclaims its quality.

To his great surprise, Apu goes to the village a bachelor and returns a married man; it turns out the bridegroom is mad and Apu, again giving in to his friend Pulu, agrees to take his place, lest Aparna be cursed by orthodox Hindu tradition to remain unmarried for life. For a brief, sweet spell, Apu and Aparna live in his primitive room in Calcutta. He works as a clerk (a job got for him by Pulu), she keeps house. They are utterly absorbed in one another. When she leaves him to have their child in her village, Apu drifts blissfully through his dreary office routine awaiting the moment of togetherness again. Instead, Aparna dies, leaving a baby son. Apu is laid waste by grief, contemplates suicide, and leaves Calcutta.

Wandering by the coast, in the forest and in the mountains, he renounces his former life, his novel, and Kajal, the son he has not seen. For five years he disappears until Pulu again tracks him down – this time working in an isolated mining settlement. The meeting with Pulu stirs old and poignant memories. Apu feels driven to make contact with Kajal. Although the boy has grown up wild and withdrawn and at first distrusts the strange bearded man who woos him, a tentative bond eventually forms between them. In a searing finale, Apu sweeps the little boy into his arms and, united, they set off for Calcutta.

The relationship of the second film to Banerji's two novels is much closer than that of the third film to the second novel, as already remarked. In *Aparajito*, Banerji's depiction of the mother-son conflict took strong hold of Ray's imagination from the start, partly because of his own complex relationship with his widowed mother, who had encouraged his artistic talents but discouraged him from giving up his safe job in advertising to become a film-maker after 1950. The Apu–Sarbajaya relationship 'had some echoes on a purely psychological plane', said a reticent Ray. Although he would not lose his own mother until 1960, he was gripped by what he called a 'daring and profound revelation' by Banerji in the novel: 'For some time after Sarbajaya's death Apu became familiar with a strange sensation ... his immediate reaction had been one of pleasure, like a surge of release ... a delight in the breaking of bonds ... There was no doubt he loved his mother, but the news of her death had at first brought him pleasure – he couldn't avoid that truth.' The latter portion of the film *Aparajito* consisted, said Ray, 'of improvisations on that extraordinarily revealing statement.'

The Apu of the third film is a nobler creation than the Apu of the novel. Ray dispenses with some of his contradictions, attenuates his narcissism and draws him as someone of heightened sensitivity and refined emotion – more of an artist than Banerji's Apu. In the novel, Apu is content to leave Aparna in the village for about a year after their marriage; and when she dies in childbirth, he reacts to the news in Calcutta with a calmness that surprises even himself, and continues dully with his office life for some while. Ray, on the other hand, was 'very touched by the fact that although it's an arranged marriage they fall in love', and decided to emphasise this in the film. When Aparna dies in *The World of Apu*, by contrast, Apu lashes out at her brother in grief, attempts suicide and abruptly abandons the city.

The author's Apu also has a much wider contact with girls before he meets Aparna than does Ray's. While still a boy in Benares, the Apu of the last part of *Pather Panchali* becomes attached to Lila, the privileged grand-daughter of the rich man his mother works for, with an affection she reciprocates. When he goes back to the village, he feels Lila's absence very strongly. Later, Apu continues to visit Lila in Calcutta occasionally, and she is part of the influence of the city in alienating Apu from his mother. After Aparna's death he comes close to her again; at one point, she offers to sponsor the publication of Apu's novel, which has been rejected by conventional publishers. However, Apu's relationship with Lila is never an affair in the usual sense of a physical passion. According to the novel, 'Lila was his childhood companion; he felt a tender affection for her, compassion and a strong bond of friendship, almost as if she was his sister.' In Ray's view, 'They have nice conversations but it never amounts to any deep relationship.'

Nonetheless, he allowed, 'Bibhutibhusan had laid so much stress on the Apu–Lila relationship that I was a bit worried about leaving her out altogether.' Ray therefore tried, but failed, to find a suitable girl to play Lila in *Aparajito*; after two mismatches, his third actress was abducted from him on the first day of shooting by her irate fiancé. Reluctantly, Ray wrote Lila out of the script, which meant, of course, that she was out of the third film too. 'I'm never sure whether Apu's attachment to the city without the element of the girlfriend is strong enough,' Ray said in the 1980s; 'the pull that the city exerts is a bit abstract I think, and yet ... watching *Aparajito* recently I didn't feel the absence of Lila at all.' His own experience in his formative years may have influenced him here; he never had a girlfriend, and the only girls he knew well were his various cousins, including Bijoya, whom he early on decided to marry.

A less radical change to the novel in the second film is its treatment of Benares and its unique ghats leading down to the Ganges. The first section of the film is a miraculous evocation of the city's atmosphere through the eyes of a newcoming family, Apu in particular, conveyed largely without the use of words. While some of these visual aspects of the city are described in the novel, most are not. For example, there is not a single sentence referring to the pigeons or monkeys that are such a feature of life in Benares and of Ray's film – perhaps because Banerji took them for granted in the minds of his Bengali readers. The film's celebrated scene following the death rattle of Harihar and the last-minute giving of Ganges water by Apu at the insistence of Sarbajaya, of a flock of pigeons suddenly taking flight and wheeling in the dawn sky above Benares, is therefore entirely the creation of Ray. As is the scene of a curious Apu throwing food to a crowd of monkeys in a Hindu temple, whilst eagerly observing the animals' inimitable cavortings. Ray deliberately wrote the Benares scenes of the film while staying in Benares and kept a fascinating diary in which he described these monkeys:

> *March 4* [1956] – Visited the Durga Temple. People who come here with the intent of offering a prayer to the deity usually do so with half a mind, the other half being on the

monkeys. These animals go about the place as if they owned it. Irresistibly funny, they sometimes go for your bag of peanuts with alarming viciousness. But when they swing from the bell-ropes and perform an impromptu *carillon*, the sight and sound are no longer merely comic.

Rich possibility of a scene here, with Apu.

Other significant changes to the novel in the Benares section of the film involve human relationships. The young Lila is omitted, as already mentioned. Although Apu is seen with young male friends, much of the time he wanders the streets and bathing ghats alone, nor does he attend a city school. Ray intensifies Sarbajaya's isolation, too, presumably for dramatic purposes. In the novel, she develops a friendship with a Punjabi woman who lives upstairs with her family and is present at Harihar's deathbed; in the film, the woman is just an acquaintance, and only Apu witnesses the death. After she becomes a cook, Sarbajaya decides to leave the household because someone unjustly canes Apu as a punishment; in the film, her decision is provoked purely by her catching sight of her cherished son preparing a tobacco pipe for the household, like a servant working for his master.

The rest of the second film – set in the village of Sarbajaya's aged relative Bhabataran and then in Calcutta – is largely faithful to the novel, in spirit if not in detail. 'Why did the unknown hold such attraction for him?' Sarbajaya asks herself about Apu in the novel. This gulf in comprehension between mother and son defines the film too. Apart from the fact that in the film Apu is not sent away from the village to board at a secondary school, and that his love is for science rather than the humanities, the other main change from the novel is that Apu has somewhat more money, and experiences less hardship, in the film. Banerji's Apu, unlike Ray's, is often at starvation level while studying in Calcutta. Perhaps Ray felt that too grim a depiction of want would unbalance the film and also drive away his audience, as well as being inconsistent with Banerji's fundamentally optimistic outlook. (In Ray's later famine film, *Distant Thunder*, also based on a novel by Banerji, only one corpse is actually shown on screen.)

With the final film, *The World of Apu*, there is little point in comparing it with the novel *Aparajito* in any detail. Both film and novel centre on the marriage of Apu and Aparna, accidentally arranged by Pulu, Apu's friend and Aparna's cousin; but otherwise the two works differ radically in story, structure and mood. Consider a few crucial examples. Apu's impoverished garret above the steam and whistles of the railway yard, which opens the film, was entirely Ray's vivid creation, as was the pivotal scene there in which an indignant Pulu bursts in and takes Apu out for a meal. In the film, from the beginning Apu is already writing an autobiographical novel, which Pulu reads in manuscript before he introduces his friend to Aparna, and which Apu discards in disillusion after the death of Aparna; in Banerji's novel, Apu begins writing his novel well *after* the death of Aparna, which his childhood friend Lila enthusiastically reads before it is eventually published. In the film, when Aparna's brother brings news of her death to Apu, a grief-stricken Apu punches him in the face; in the novel it is the brother who breaks down, and Apu who calmly asks him questions about his wife's death. Lastly, in the film, Apu's son Kajal, whom he abandons after Aparna's death, at first truculently rejects his unknown father's overtures; whereas in the novel, Apu is immediately embraced by Kajal with open arms.

Even the psychology of the wedding of Apu and Aparna is very different in the film from that in the novel. In both cases, the first bridegroom turns out to be mad. But in the film when Pulu, desperate to help his young cousin, approaches Apu on the river-bank and asks him to wed Aparna instead, Apu sharply rejects him with the words: 'Are you still living in the Dark Ages?' Then, upon reflection, observing the forlorn wedding preparations, Apu does agree; he puts it to Pulu in a very oblique way typical of Ray – by asking if Pulu can really get him the job he had earlier promised and which Apu had rejected as too routine – 'because any direct statement like "OK, I agree to marry your cousin" would have sounded terrible,' said Ray. 'A western viewer ignorant of orthodox Hindu customs must find the episode highly bizarre', he further commented. 'But since Apu himself finds it so, and since his action is prompted by compassion, the viewer accepts it on moral grounds, though given no opportunity to weigh the pros and cons of a seemingly irrational practice.' That this is true is chiefly because Ray, with his Brahmo family background and its rejection of orthodox Hinduism, could not accept Banerji's version of Apu's marriage and therefore 'reformed' it. In the novel, Apu sleeps upstairs and is woken by Pulu in the middle of the night with the news about the mad bridegroom; quickly he falls in with Pulu's rescue plan: 'Very well, just tell me what I have to do' – which really *would* have left a western viewer bemused.

Banerji and his novels were Hindu to the core – 'Harihar Ray was a Brahmin' is the opening sentence of *Pather Panchali* – unlike his interpreter Ray and his films. In adapting the two novels *Pather Panchali* and *Aparajito* to make the Apu Trilogy, Ray contrived to retain the Hindu details and atmosphere familiar to Bengali and Indian viewers, while emphasising a strong and simple theme about a boy's struggle to become a man, to which anyone can relate, anywhere in the world. Ray's Apu, unlike Banerji's original creation, is truly 'an inhabitant of the universe', not a country cousin.

3

An Epic in Production: Making the Apu Trilogy

Pather Panchali never had a proper script. Unlike every other Ray film, there was no red, cloth-bound shooting notebook for it. Instead, Ray had the treatment that he had started on board ship from London in October 1950 and, from early 1952, a sheaf of sketches of the most important shots in black ink which he deposited, years later, at the Cinémathèque in Paris. Most of the film's dialogue, three-quarters of it from Bibhutibhusan Banerji's novel, he kept in his head. By showing producers these vivid sketches, which were unheard of in Bengali film-making, and telling them the story, he hoped to raise interest in a film with him as its director.

First, though, he took his treatment to Banerji's young widow – whose husband had unexpectedly died on 1 November, just after Ray's return from London – to persuade her to part with the rights to the novel. She received him warmly, being an admirer of both his grandfather Upendrakisore's and his father Sukumar's work, and of Satyajit's cover designs and his illustrations for the abridged edition of *Pather Panchali*. She said that her late husband had always believed his writing had film potential but that no one had seemed interested. She gave her agreement

Sketch by Ray for script of *Pather Panchali*, 1952, showing Apu and Durga in the fields with the train

in principle; however no financial arrangements were discussed. When the news was announced in the Calcutta newspapers, she received letters from friends rebuking her for her faith in an unknown; but, fortunately for Ray, she stuck by him throughout the film's long and painful gestation.

Like Jean Renoir, who touted the script of *La Grande Illusion* round French producers for three years (often with Jean Gabin, his chief draw, rather than a famous story, in tow), Ray spent nearly two years trying to sell his film on the back of the novel's fame. Most of the potential producers who half-listened to him could not see beyond the fact that he offered none of the entertainment traditionally part of Bengali films; a few who had more imagination nonetheless insisted on a co-director. 'Who would come to see an old hag like that?' 'Where was the love interest?' 'Why were there no songs?' – these were some of the reactions. 'They were stupid people,' remarked Ray in the 1980s. 'They believed only in a certain kind of commercial cinema. But one kept hoping that presented with something fresh and original and affecting, they would change.'

One of them, who undoubtedly perceived commercial possibilities in the story if conventionally done, played a trick on Ray. This man met him, heard him out, and suggested a further meeting a week later to draw up a contract. In the meantime the producer paid a visit to Mrs Banerji with a proposal that the successful director Debaki Bose do the film and made a large offer for the rights. She turned him down.

Ray got only one genuine offer, and that fell through when the producer's then-current film opened and failed. But the man who had arranged this meeting, Anil Chowdhury, joined the small group of people around Ray (including Subrata Mitra, his future cameraman, and Bansi Chandragupta, his future art director) who would make *Pather Panchali* possible. Chowdhury became production controller of this and all subsequent films by Ray.

In mid-1952, Chowdhury recalled Ray's declaring to him in his office at Keymer's that he could live in limbo no longer. Four years before, he had written to his English friend Norman Clare: 'It looks as if I'll have to rot and be exploited in Keymer's for some time [yet].' He now decided to borrow around 7,000 rupees against his life insurance policy and another 10,000 rupees from his relatives and friends, to shoot enough footage to persuade a producer to back the whole film. If no one would, he said to Chowdhury, he would have to remain a commercial artist forever.

Ray was determined to prove the film industry's professionals wrong in their conviction that outdoors shooting with amateur actors was unworkable. He and Mitra hired an old 16mm camera and set off one weekend for Gopalnagar, the village on which Banerji had based his fictional one. It was the rainy season and they had to squelch through knee-deep mud to get there. They filmed in 'the dim light of a mango grove, in pouring rain and in the falling light of dusk.' Every shot came out.

But the village itself Ray considered to be insufficiently photogenic. So his next problem was to find a location suitable for the daytime scenes in the film (the night-time ones were always intended to be shot in a studio). Besides a house of the right general layout and decay to fit Harihar Ray's, the story demanded a pond nearby, a river, fields and a railway line. In the event, Ray settled for two locations: the ruined house and pond in the village of Boral only six miles from the centre of Calcutta, and the fields (where Apu and Durga run together) with the railway line about 100 miles away. The river he decided to drop. After negotiations with the owner of the house, 'a nasty old man' bedridden in Calcutta to whom they had to pay 50 rupees every month for the next two and a half years, Chandragupta set to work on an extensive conversion.

They began shooting on 27 October 1952, in the fields. Ray felt that the scene in which Apu chases Durga through a field of white *kash* (similar to pampas grass) and sees a train for the first time would make a fine come-on for a producer. But he did not appreciate just how tough a target he had set himself as a director. Some of the lessons it taught him he recorded in various articles in his book *Our Films Their Films*; they concern, mostly, the correct use of camera and lenses. 'The moment you are on the set the three-legged instrument takes charge. Problems come thick and fast', he wrote. 'Where to place the camera? High or low? Near or far? On the dolly or on the ground? Is the 35 OK or would you rather move back and use the 50? Get too close to the action and the emotion of the scene spills over; get too far back and the thing becomes cold and remote. To each problem that arises you must find a quick answer. If you delay, the sun shifts and makes nonsense of your light continuity.'

But one lesson involved the direction of Apu. The boy was expected to walk haltingly through the *kash* as if on the lookout for Durga. 'Little did I know then that it was twice as hard to achieve impeccability in a shot like that than in a shot of, say, charging cavalry.' It did not help that Subir Banerji as Apu was a decidedly unresponsive actor. 'He looked so right,' Ray said later, 'but he couldn't act at all; he was also inattentive.' Ray's solution in the end was to lay small obstacles in the boy's path for him

Pather Panchali: Apu and Durga

to measure his progress by, and to have three assistants hiding in the *kash* on either side who would call the boy at prearranged moments. Ray's perception of the way that De Sica handled the father in *Bicycle Thieves* (rather than the boy) helped to give him the confidence to direct his child actor as a puppet too.

In his first film Ray confessed he felt 'safer with non-actors', but it would be wrong to assume, as many have done, that all the actors in *Pather Panchali* had no prior experience. When Ray attended a seminar in the United States in 1958, organised by Robert Flaherty's widow who greatly admired *Pather Panchali*, he had to use a lot of persuasion to convince her he had been right to use non-villagers in the film – unlike Flaherty's documentaries on pre-industrial cultures such as *Nanook of the North*. In fact, of the major characters, Indir, Harihar, the two women neighbours and the grocer–schoolmaster, were all played by professionals, while Karuna Banerji (Sarbajaya) and Uma Das Gupta (Durga) had had experience on the stage; only the smaller roles – such as the old men who visit Harihar at the end of the film to persuade him to stay in the village – were played by the villagers of Boral.

To find Apu, Ray had advertised in newspapers asking five- to seven-year-old boys to come and see him. Hundreds turned up – even a girl, whose parents had had a salon cut her hair and powder her shoulders – but the choice eventually fell on a boy whom Ray's wife spotted playing on the roof next to the flat they were now renting in south Calcutta. The girl who would play Durga was discovered by a friend of Ray who knew the headmistress of a girls' school in Calcutta. When Uma Das Gupta met Ray she thought she was auditioning for a stage play. She put on a pearl necklace of which she was proud. 'The first remark Manikda [Ray] made was that I would have to take it off.' Karuna Banerji (the mother in real life of Runki Banerji, the young Durga in the early part of the film) was suggested for the part of Sarbajaya by her husband Subrata, a friend of Ray and his colleague in advertising at Keymer's. Karuna was not enthusiastic and wrote to

Ray saying so, suggesting another actress. Although she had acted a good deal in the Indian People's Theatre Association (IPTA) – the federation of groups formed throughout India in the early 1940s to which creative people of all kinds were drawn – she was fairly conventional in her view of cinema acting as unsuitable for respectable women. Family pressure persuaded her otherwise. As Sarbajaya, Karuna never felt any difficulty in identifying herself with a village housewife living in poverty. Although her life had been spent in cities (like Ray himself), she had been born in a large family in East Bengal and, like the Ray family of Sukumar's generation, she used to return to her ancestral village at festival time when she was growing up.

But of all Ray's casting in *Pather Panchali*, his most inspired choices must be Tulsi Chakravarti as the grocer–schoolmaster, and Chunibala Devi as Indir, the film's 'most outstanding performance' in Ray's view and that of many others (including myself). Chakravarti, at the time Ray cast him, was very well known in Bengal for a kind of broad comic acting that Ray did not much care for. He had run away from home when he was fifteen or sixteen and joined a circus party where he became a trapeze artist. Later, after acting in silent films, he joined the payroll of New Theatres (where Ray's uncle Nitin Bose was a director) and played bit-parts like landlords, moneylenders and grocers. Ray had felt a marvellous expressiveness in his face and sensed that he was being wasted. He was delighted when Chakravarti agreed to play in *Pather Panchali*; 'I was a nobody at that time – in the film business anyway,' Ray said. At the end of the first day's shooting, Chakravarti told him, 'I've never had so much interesting business.' A few years later, not long before his death, he gave one of the best performances ever delivered in a Ray film, as the humble clerk who finds the philosopher's stone and is transformed overnight into a nouveau riche in *The Philosopher's Stone/Paras Pathar*.

The early shots of *Pather Panchali* had already been taken before Ray located an old woman capable of playing Indir; it surprised him to the end of his life to think that he could have been

Ray rehearsing Chunibala Devi in *Pather Panchali*

so heedless of the risk he was running. '[When] I cast my mind back to those days', he wrote in his autobiography, 'I am struck by a signal lack of professionalism on our part.' During the shooting he often found himself thinking that *Pather Panchali* could not have happened without Chunibala. Banerji's description of the old woman was a tall order to fulfil: '75, sunken cheeks, slightly crooked at the waist and hunched forward – she cannot see things at a distance as she once could.' Not that Calcutta lacked for such old women, but the part also required acting ability, stamina and a good memory. Ray's chances were not improved by the fact that he intended using no make-up, as his newspaper advertisements made clear; he was always against making up a younger actress for the part.

He heard about Chunibala Devi from the professional actress Reba Devi (no relation – 'Devi' simply indicates a mature, generally married woman), who played the part of Sejbou, the shrewish neighbour in *Pather Panchali*. It turned out that Chunibala was the mother of a well-known actress, though unmarried. In 1953, she was about 80 years old and had been on the stage for some 30 years in the first decades of the century, when she also acted in silent films. Since then she had been more or less retired.

Ray paid a visit to Chunibala's house in a red-light district of north Calcutta. He was soon satisfied. 'But what part can I play at the age of 80?' asked Chunibala. 'That of an 80-year-old woman,' Ray replied. 'I don't have an answer to that. Ha ha!' she chuckled. When asked if she could recite a rhyme, Chunibala recalled many more lines of a particular lullaby than Ray himself knew. And when asked if she were capable of rising at six o'clock, travelling fifteen miles to the location by taxi, standing up to a day's shooting followed by the journey back, she was quite certain she was. The only condition she made, apart from a small salary, was that she should be provided with her daily dose of opium. The one day she missed it, she fainted.

From the beginning, Chunibala grasped Ray's intention that the film should display no artifice. 'She was constantly aware that authenticity was the touchstone of her performance', he wrote. She was careful to wear her widow's sari with its torn portions knotted, as a poor woman in her position would do. After a while the garment became really ragged and barely covered her decently. When word of her feelings reached Ray, he asked for a new piece of cloth to be provided for her with fewer holes in it. This was done, but when Chunibala next appeared on set she was still wearing the old sari. Her memory for continuity was formidable. Ray recalled that she often picked up details he had missed, with comments like: 'That time it was my right hand which was wet', 'Wait, there was no sweat on my face before', 'In this shot my shawl wouldn't be covering me', 'Was my bundle in my right hand? No, it was in my left. My brass pot was in my right.'

The village of Boral provided most of the remaining actors. Although Ray had an introduction to someone in the village, the initial reaction to him and his team was not very friendly, at least among the older villagers. This quite soon improved though, as the conversion of the ruined house progressed and shooting began using some of the locals. One incident was particularly effective in thawing the atmosphere. Ray had seen someone in the village whom he wanted to play the bald-headed villager woken by the first drop of monsoon rain on his pate, but he did not know the man's name. So he scribbled a quick sketch of him. 'Hari Babu!' the villagers shouted and promptly fetched him. 'I think this feat brought me more acclaim than anything else I had done in the years we spent in Boral', joked Ray in his autobiography.

The enthusiasm that comes from breaking new ground pervaded the production. In the words of Subrata Banerji, who watched some of the shooting, 'Satyajit seemed a different person. He was rarely withdrawn. There was an abandon about him. The warmth in his relations with others that was rarely evident came out clearly... He could easily set the mood for an occasion by his own behaviour. He seemed to live through the experiences of the characters he was creating for his film and so did the individuals who portrayed the parts.' Banerji's wife Karuna agreed, as did the great majority of those who acted for Ray; their most frequent observation was, that they 'never felt they were acting'.

There was one person in Boral who intrigued Ray more than any other, though he does not appear in *Pather Panchali*. He was the first to greet them the day they arrived to shoot. He called out loudly: 'The film people are 'ere! Watch out! Reach for your spears, reach for your spears!' Indeed he believed that the villagers were equally untrustworthy, as he confided when he came to know Ray and his team a bit better. They had cheated him of land, he said, and he had ancient deeds to prove it. He believed that deceit was in the very marrow of Boral. Once he told Ray: 'Imagine ten men walking along a village path in single file on a totally moonless night. Not one of them has brought a lamp – they're that mean. The leading man falls into a hole, and as he does so, he keeps himself to himself – he doesn't warn the others. And so every one of them falls into the hole and none of them lets out a peep for fear of benefiting the others. That's what they're like here in Boral.' He had names for many of them too, reckoning Churchill and Hitler among his neighbours. He would see a certain man cycling by and say, quite seriously: 'That's Roosevelt. He hasn't forgotten his tricks. What a devilish fellow!' Subodhda, as this crackpot was called, must have helped Ray create his memorable madman a few years later in *The Postmaster*. About five years after he left Boral, Ray had occasion to return there. He felt disappointed to find Subodhda sane. Gone were his ancient land deeds and his accusations. His only vaguely interesting remark was: 'I wish you'd come in the mango season. They were good this year.'

The shooting in Boral did not begin until early 1953. There had been a gap of some months after those first shots in the field of *kash*, in which Ray had made a renewed effort to interest producers in his footage. In the meantime, in late 1952, there

Ray on location in Boral near Calcutta, while shooting *Pather Panchali*, with actress Karuna Banerji and cameraman Subrata Mitra

had come encouragement of a different sort: the first international film festival to be held in India. Satyajit and his friends rushed from cinema to cinema, seeing about four films a day for a fortnight. 'Mercifully,' remarked Ray, 'there were no jurors, no prizes, no seminars, few parties, and only a handful of visiting celebrities.' The future Bengali director Mrinal Sen, who was then a medical representative, noted in his diary:

10 a.m.–12 noon	Visiting doctors: 4 will do.
3 p.m.	At Purna Theatre: *Rome, Open City* by Roberto Rossellini.
6 p.m.	At Menoka: *Jour de Fête* by Jacques Tati.
9 p.m.	At Light House: *Miracle in Milan* by Vittorio de Sica.

The film that made the biggest impression on Ray and his friends was Akira Kurosawa's *Rashomon*. They knew of its rave reviews at the Venice Film Festival the previous year. Ray saw it three times on consecutive days 'and wondered each time if there was another film anywhere which gave such sustained and dazzling proof of a director's command over every aspect of film-making.' He was thrilled by the camerawork in the woodcutter's journey through the forest, 'cut with axe-edge precision'.

The success of the unknown Kurosawa in the West gave further impetus to Ray's fledgling ambitions and suggested that *Pather Panchali* might one day find a western audience too. A film made in India at that time, which Ray later described as a 'landmark', also encouraged him, since it was shot partly on location, concerned a peasant family, and involved few songs and no dances. This was Bimal Roy's *Two Acres of Land/Do Bigha Zamin*, which won the Prix International at the 1954 Cannes Film Festival.

Seeing Ray's pilot footage, a producer called Rana Dutta eventually came forward and advanced enough money for him to shoot some scenes in Boral. No one involved could be paid, bar one assistant, Santi Chatterji (who remained with Ray until his death), and, among the cast, Chunibala Devi. Things were run on such a slender shoestring that the production controller Chowdhury took to sleeping in taxis for lack of an alarm clock; the taxi-driver simply parked his vehicle on a tramway and woke up as soon as the first tram of the day appeared!

Shooting was in progress when some of Dutta's films opened and failed. There was no money now even to buy lunch. Chowdhury turned, in desperation, to Ray's wife Bijoya, who agreed to pawn some of her jewellery, without consulting her husband. It realised 1,300 rupees. They had to get the jewellery back later, in exchange for some belonging to Chowdhury's sister, so that Bijoya could wear it at a ceremony just before the birth of her son Sandip in September 1953; neither Bijoya nor Satyajit wanted his mother to discover what she had done for the sake of the film. (They later found out that Suprabha Ray already knew but had kept the secret to herself.)

The nadir of Ray's hopes was reached in the latter part of 1953 and early 1954. He had shown his 4,000 feet of edited footage to just about every producer in Bengal, and they had been 'completely apathetic'. In several attempts to find producers he had paid middle men with money raised by selling his art books and records, without telling even his wife, and had been cheated. The only bright spot was his absolute conviction that he was doing something important, certainly in Indian films, and perhaps internationally too. 'The rushes told us that. The rushes told us that the children were behaving marvellously and the old woman was an absolute stunner. Nobody had ever seen such an old woman in an Indian film before.'

Ray's friends at the coffee house and the British managers at Keymer's also helped to maintain his morale. He had been showing them stills as the work progressed, which clearly excited them. One still – a three-shot of Sarbajaya and Durga getting Apu ready for school – was selected in early 1954 for Edward Steichen's great exhibition *The Family of Man*. Ray also showed rushes to some of his friends, one of whom told him: 'This is India's first adult film.'

The Keymer's managers, in particular J. B. R. Nicholson, permitted Ray, who was the jewel in their crown, to take time off to shoot his film as he saw fit. On occasions this leave was even paid. The manager of the Bombay branch, Robert Hardcastle, recalled visiting Calcutta on business some time in 1953–54 and seeing Ray's sketches at the insistence of the Calcutta manager. He was very struck by 'their power and atmosphere'. Shooting was at that time suspended and Ray told Hardcastle that one of his main anxieties was that his elderly actress would die.

The gap in the shooting lasted almost a year. In the early months of 1954 two sources of help appeared, one foreign, the other indigenous. Monroe Wheeler of New York's Museum of Modern Art turned up in Calcutta in February in pursuit of materials for an exhibition of Indian textiles and ornaments. He got to hear of the film and visited Ray at his office. The stills he saw there thrilled him. 'He felt it was very high quality lighting, composition, faces, textures and so on,' said Ray. 'That gave him the notion it would be a film worth showing at his festival.' Together, they paid a visit to Tagore's Shantiniketan, which has a strong craft tradition that interested Wheeler. He came to know Ray quite well, and 'I think he got the impression I would come up with something exciting. "Do you think you could let us have this film for our exhibition?" he asked. "That's a year from now."' – May 1955. Ray could hardly believe his ears.

The second source was the Government of West Bengal, whose chief minister was then an energetic figure from a Brahmo family, Dr B. C. Roy, who had earlier been Mahatma Gandhi's physician and friend. Roy had helped Uday Shankar fund his pioneering film *Kalpana* in 1948. Ray's mother had a woman friend with influence over Roy. Though very dubious about film-making as a way of life, she had never doubted her son's artistic talent, and was distressed by the dashing of his hopes in 1953; so she arranged for her friend to see the edited footage.

The friend then persuaded the chief minister to meet Ray. Roy was sympathetic but did not know Banerji's novel and from the beginning understood the film to be more documentary than drama. Noting that the script had a tragic ending – with Apu's family leaving the village – he asked Ray if he could change the ending and have the family stay and rebuild their house. 'Can't you inject a message that would go in favour of our work on community development?' asked the chief minister. One of Ray's supporters at the meeting countered by saying that the Banerji family and the Bengali public would object to changing a literary classic. Apparently accepting this argument, Roy directed his officials in the Home Publicity Department to examine the costs of backing *Pather Panchali* as a Community Development Project, after they had viewed Ray's footage.

They knew little about the novel either, and cared not at all about the film. One of them, watching the magical scene in which the little procession of sweet-seller, Durga, Apu and a village dog is reflected upside-down in a pond, shouted out that the film was running backwards! The head of the department reported privately to the chief minister: 'My impression is that even when exploited, this picture will not pay as much as is being invested in it. *Pather Panchali* is rather dull and slow-moving. It is a story of a typical Bengali family suffering privation and family embarrassments, but at no point does it offer a solution or an attempt to better the lot of the people and rebuild the structure of their society.' Ray's experience with these philistine officials in 1954 and after would be one of pure frustration.

Fortunately, a well-known playwright, Manmatha Roy, also saw the footage along with the officials and reported on it ecstatically. Contracts were drawn up by the government, in which Mrs Banerji was paid for the film rights to the novel and the producer Rana Dutta for the money he had already invested; but Ray himself received nothing. Nothing was put in writing about foreign rights either, although Ray made a verbal agreement with the Home Publicity Department head that he would share in these, should the film be sold abroad, as Ray now suspected might happen. This was later overlooked by the government – which meant that Ray received no income whatsoever from *Pather Panchali*. 'They get the money but I got the fame,' he told his first biographer Marie Seton a few years later.

The most tiresome aspect of this relationship was that Ray's team had to render accounts for each stage of the shooting, before the government would release the next instalment of money. 'It was very unpleasant,' he remembered. 'It meant, for one thing, that we missed the rainy season, and we had to shoot the rain scenes in October. Throughout the rainy season we had no money. It meant going to the location every day with the entire crew and cast and just waiting. There were days and days of waiting and doing nothing... It was a kind of picnic, but not a very pleasant picnic. We would keep looking at the sky and at little patches of cloud which wouldn't produce any rain.'

If it is amazing that they were able to make such an authentic film under these conditions, it is a miracle that they did not fall foul of other, totally intransigent obstacles. Three miracles to be precise, according to Ray: 'One, Apu's voice did not break. Two, Durga did not grow up. Three, Indir Thakrun did not die.'

With hindsight, Ray came to see some advantages in the delays. First, he learnt to assess the length of a scene in scenario form, and secondly, to edit a film in sections, as it was shot, thus saving time later. This way of editing soon became a habit with him, even after he could afford to wait until he had finished shooting. More important, he learnt a lot about technique from a severe scrutiny of the material he had shot before being forced to stop, which was about half the film, and he applied this hard-won knowledge in shooting the second half. Until the end of his days he would feel, justifiably, that the first half of *Pather Panchali* needed cutting, because 'the pace sometimes falters... And there are certain things we couldn't do anything about, like camera placements. I don't think the relationship of the three little cottages [in Harihar's house] is very clear in the

Shooting *Pather Panchali* in Boral near Calcutta

film. You have to choose a master-angle, which you keep repeating so that people get their bearings. If you keep changing the camera angle, it becomes very confusing. In your mind the plan is very clear but to make it clear on the screen you have to use certain devices which we didn't know at that time.'

Throughout the protracted production process of *Pather Panchali*, the shooting was a mixture of the premeditated and the improvised. It is quite clear from Ray's initial sheaf of sketches done in 1952 how much he improved his scenario by his long exposure to the locations themselves. All the elements in the opening sequence of the film – little Durga picking up fruit and skipping home to Indir Thakrun, Sarbajaya drawing water wearily from the well with her suspicious neighbour Sejbou watching her and then ticking off Durga for stealing – are there in the initial sketches, but in the film the human inter-relationships are made more graphic and the scene richer, because the neighbour actually *sees* Durga take a fruit and the girl's mother Sarbajaya is forced to overhear her caustic comments.

One of the premeditated sequences was the passing away of Indir. Her solitary death, followed by the children discovering her corpse, was entirely Ray's invention; as Durga playfully shakes her squatting form, it crashes over and her head hits the ground with a sickening thud. This is the only scene at which Chunibala demurred – not because of the potential injury but because she felt Indir's death at the village shrine, as it is in the novel, to be more appropriate. Ray persuaded her both to do the scene his way and not to worry about hurting herself. He would always remember the mixture of elation and exhaustion on her face after taking this shot.

For her funeral, which is not described in the novel, Ray again decided to be unconventional by avoiding the usual Hindu chant; in his experience there were always some people in an Indian audience who would feel obliged to join in. His aim was to invest the scene with beauty as well as sadness, rather than just making it grim. So he decided to have Indir's body carried out on a bier

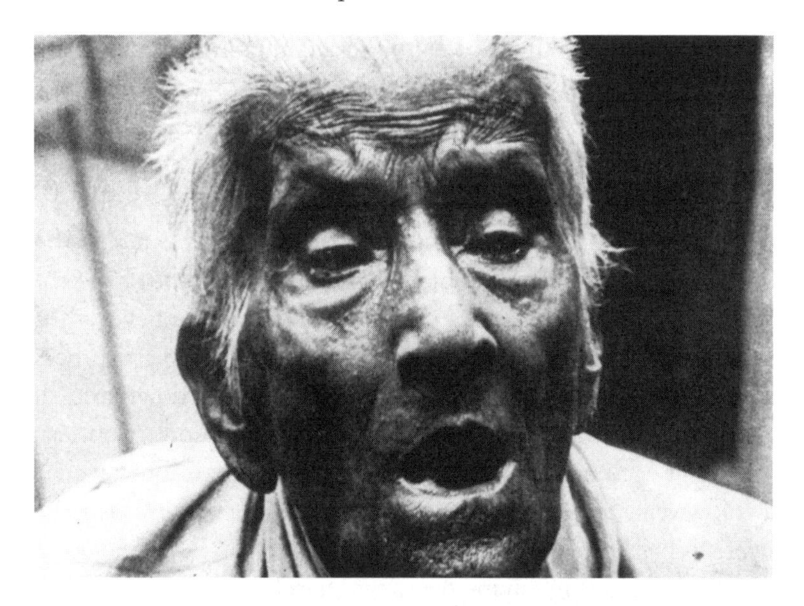

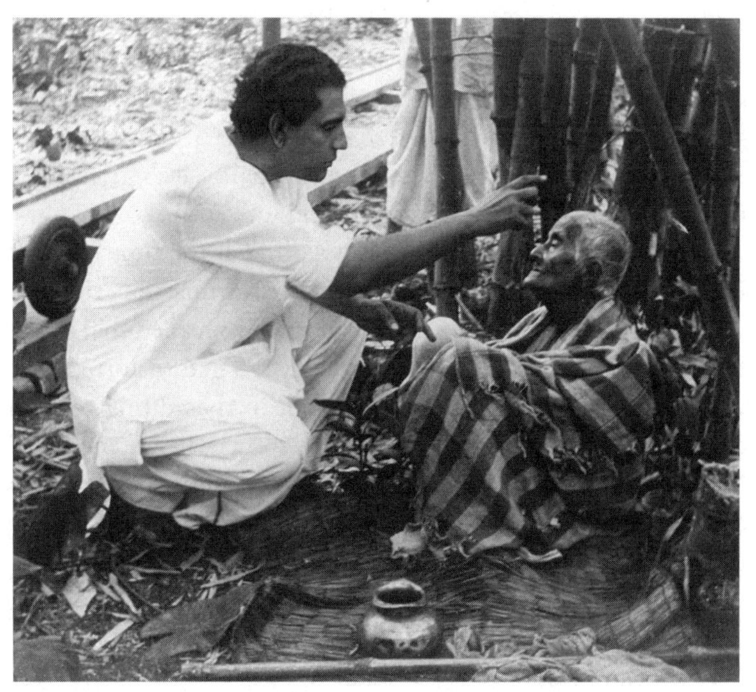

Pather Panchali: Indir Thakrun; Ray directs Chunibala Devi in the scene of Indir's death at sunrise down a village path, to the accompaniment of her own familiar mournful song.

At five in the morning they were standing ready to shoot. When Chunibala Devi arrived by taxi Ray plucked up his courage and broke the news to the old lady: 'Today we will carry you out on a bier.' She was not in the least put out. So they spread a mat on a bamboo bier, covered her with the shawl that in the story she begs from a neighbour, and fastened everything securely with rope. There was a rehearsal and the funeral procession began. The shot complete, the bier was put down and the ropes untied. But Chunibala did not stir. The production team looked at each other. What could have happened? They were in a cold sweat. Suddenly they heard Chunibala's voice: 'Is the shot over? Why didn't anyone tell me? I'm still lying here dead'!

Another scene involving death was handled with less certainty by Ray. This is the return of Harihar to find his house ruined and his daughter dead, followed by Sarbajaya's breakdown. Her grief-stricken wail is expressed not by her own voice but by a stringed instrument, the *tarshehnai*, playing a passage of high notes; the startling effect is to intensify Sarbajaya's grief and to transform it into something nobler and universal.

This substitution was not in Ray's mind at the time of shooting. The day before, he had written for Karuna Banerji a note about the situation, and on the day itself she recalled that he told her: 'Don't be afraid to distort your face. If it gets distorted, don't worry, just be normal, as it comes.' But in the editing room he came to feel that the scene required a 'special, heightened quality' not accessible to the naked voice. After adding the music he considered keeping Karuna's crying sound too but decided it was ineffective in combination. He did not tell his actress, though; when she first saw the film, she jerked forward in surprise at that point. But although the change disappointed her then, she soon felt that Ray's notion was a wonderful one.

A tiny detail from that same sequence gives a good idea of how definite Ray's intentions in his first film normally were. When

Sarbajaya first hears Harihar calling out for his children, she is vacantly squatting, with her arm and a white bangle pressed against her cheek. Involuntarily, she reacts to her husband's voice and moves her arm; the bangle slips down slightly. The indifference of her gesture suggests just how indifferent to the world she has become. It took Ray seven takes to get the bangle to move exactly as he wanted it to. (The normal number of takes in *Pather Panchali* was a highly economical one or two.)

He was also determined to get a typical village dog to trot along behind Durga and Apu as they follow the sweet-seller. The dog he chose was fine in rehearsal but wholly uninterested under the camera's gaze. This time it took twelve takes, about 1,000 feet of film and a tempting sweet invisibly held out behind Durga's back, to make the dog perform properly.

Of the scenes that were wholly improvised, three are outstanding. First, there are the water-skaters and dragonflies exploring the twigs, lilies and lotus leaves in the pond like Apu exploring his village; along with Ravi Shankar's sitar music, they herald the coming of the monsoon. Ray and his cameraman had shot such details of nature while idly 'picnicking', waiting for the rain required by the main shooting. The scene with the insects occurred to Ray only after the music had been composed. Secondly, there is the train rumbling away from Apu and Durga into the distance leaving a swathe of black smoke against the white *kash* flowers. Five trains were used in shooting the scene. After the last had departed, Ray noticed the unusual spectacle produced by the smoke: 'Within seconds, the camera was set up and the shot taken in fast-fading sunlight. But I think that this last-minute improvisation added a lot of beauty to the sequence.' Lastly, near the end of the film, there is Apu's discovery and concealment of the necklace once stolen from a neighbour by his now-dead sister; he throws it into the pond near the house, and the weeds first open and then close over the place where it falls, as nature hides Durga's secret. This is a delicate visual rendering of the same event described in the novel, where Apu hurls the

Ray on location in Boral near Calcutta, during the making of *Pather Panchali*

necklace into a bamboo grove – an image that Ray knew would lack impact on screen. The idea of using the pond weeds in this way struck Ray one day at the location when he and the team were again 'picnicking' during a patch of wrong weather. He was unmindfully throwing pebbles into the pond. 'Suddenly I noticed this phenomenon happening.' Instead of pebbles, why not the necklace? He almost jumped up in excitement. Along with the snake that crawls into Harihar's deserted house – which is not in the novel at all – these two touches are Ray's masterly solution to the problem of how to maintain interest after the audience knows that Apu's family is soon to leave their home.

About six months after Monroe Wheeler's visit to Calcutta, he sent emissaries to check out Ray's progress on the film. Wheeler's friend the director John Huston had actually come to India in search of locations for *The Man Who Would Be King*. The first Bengali he met as he stepped off the Pan Am flight at Calcutta's airport was Ray's friend in advertising, R. P. Gupta, who had learned of Huston's visit through his employment at J. Walter Thompson, which handled the Pan Am account. With Gupta as intermediary, Ray went to see Huston at his hotel – the same one as used by Renoir – and Huston asked if he could show him some rough cut of his film. Having warned him of the poor technical quality, Ray showed about half an hour of silent footage, avoiding scenes with substantial dialogue and concentrating on the visual highlights, especially the scene with the two children and the train. According to Ray, Huston thought it 'a fine, sincere piece of film-making' but warned him against showing too much wandering. 'The audience gets restive. They don't like to be kept waiting too long before something *happens*.' Just before his death in 1987, Huston recalled: 'I recognised the footage as the work of a great film-maker. I liked Ray enormously on first encounter. Everything he did and said supported my feelings on viewing the film.' His reaction was supported by that of another American visitor to Calcutta, Edgar Kaufmann, Jr, from the Museum of Modern Art, who reported in November 1954 to Richard Griffith, the curator of the museum's film library, that Ray's rough cut was 'a most remarkable film' – though Kaufmann seems to have seen it as some kind of documentary, showing scenes from the life of the villagers themselves, rather than a feature film.

Ray's team was now up against a very tight deadline; the film had to be finished for screening in New York in May 1955. In six months they had to complete shooting and editing it, mix the sound effects and add the soundtrack including the music, which was yet to be composed, get approval from the West Bengal Government as the film's producer, subtitle the film if there was time, and arrange for the print to go to New York. In one respect at least, Ray was fortunate; he was able to use most of the sound recorded on location. Since he and his actors were relatively unknown, they had managed to work in Boral and other locations in conditions of quiet. Never again – or only very rarely – would this occur.

The most important passages of music in *Pather Panchali* were composed by the virtuoso sitarist Ravi Shankar in early 1955 at an all-night session lasting about eleven hours until 4 a.m., because of Shankar's touring commitments. Although he was able to see only about half the film in a roughly edited version, he was deeply moved by it. He had not read the novel (according to Ray, that is – Shankar says he had), when he arrived in Calcutta, yet he knew of its merit and even before seeing the film he 'sort of hummed' for Ray a line of melody with the feeling of a folk-tune about it but which also had a certain sophistication. It became the main theme of the film, usually heard on a bamboo flute, and was 'certainly a stroke of inspiration', said Ray. During the recording itself, Ray would say: 'Now let's do a piece for such and such a portion', and Shankar and Aloke Dey, who became Ray's regular flautist, would 'go into a huddle and work out a score right then and there.' The whole recording session – for both *Pather Panchali* and later *Aparajito* – was 'hectic ... with Ravi Shankar humming, strumming, improvising and instructing at a feverish pace, and the indefatigable Aloke

Dey transcribing the composer's ideas into Indian notation and dealing out the foolscap sheets to the tense handful who had to keep plucking and bowing and thumping with scarcely a breathing space.' Shankar also composed two solo sitar pieces: a life-affirming one in raga *Desh* which is conventionally associated with the rains, and a sombre piece in raga *Todi* to follow Durga's death in the storm.

The high notes of the *tarshehnai* played when Sarbajaya bursts out in grief on the return of Harihar to their house were played by Daksinaranjan Tagore in raga *Patdeep*, chosen by Shankar. 'When we started recording,' remembered Ray, 'I kept signalling to Daksinaranjan to stay with high notes. When I got the length I wanted, I signalled to him to stop.' One or two other pieces had to be chosen by Ray after Shankar had departed. The comic twanging that so perfectly accompanies the stocky sweet-seller and his yoked sweet-pots, pursued by the hopeful children and the dog, was made by an *ektara* played by a refugee from East Bengal; the composition was by the cameraman Mitra, who also played the sitar elsewhere on the soundtrack.

'The effort to catch the Museum's deadline took on epic proportions, and my editor and I were done up to a frazzle by the end', wrote Ray. 'What turned out to be a real nightmare was the mixing of the scene in which Durga lies critically ill while a storm rages outside.' The sound effects included thunder, rain, wind, rattling doors and windows, Durga's moans, and Sarbajaya's desperate efforts to drag a trunk across the floor to stop the door flying open. 'The first attempt to mix the sounds drove us to the limits of despair. The sounds that were literally disjointed worked against and ruined the visuals which looked pure when seen without sound.' Ray's solution was to use continuous loops of sound effects – the banging of a door, falling rain, a thunder clap – the last of which had to be carefully timed to fit the flashes of lightning on the screen. 'It took until three in the morning to get the right effect. Most of the crew had fallen asleep by then except myself and the editor.'

In the last week of April 1955, they worked on a 20-hour-a-day schedule. At one point, the editor Dulal Dutta clasped Ray's feet and said he could bear the strain no longer. Production controller Chowdhury recalled that they were *living* in the Bengal Film Laboratories – not bathing, shaving, or sleeping for six or seven days. At one point, Ray's legs simply gave way beneath him as he stood up. The owner of the laboratory too stayed up all night to help them. Printing began on the evening of 29 April.

On the morning of the day of despatch, 30 April, Ray had to go out to find a suitable trunk and make official arrangements for its sending. Ray's relative and coffee-house companion Subhash Ghosal had persuaded his employer J. Walter Thompson to send the film free to New York via Pan Am. While waiting, Ray fell asleep in a chair, so that people thought he must be ill. When he returned to the laboratory, the trunk was already packed and ready to go. The team gathered round as if it were a bride about to leave her parents' home forever and go to her husband's home. The trunk was taken to the airport, and that evening departed safely for the Museum of Modern Art.

The film had no subtitles for lack of time, and Ray had not had a chance to view it, even once. The following day he had to go to Bombay on office work for Keymer's. Not until a fortnight later was he back in Calcutta and able to view the finished film in a second copy for the first time. 'It was then that I realized what a disaster it was from the sound and editing point of view', he wrote to Monroe Wheeler on 15 June. 'The first half, in particular, was full of blemishes – abrupt transitions from shot to shot, scene to scene, destroying the mood, the rhythm, the continuity; imperfect fades and dissolves; uneven print quality, and at least one scene – the stormy night – completely ruined by inadequate sound. I was so depressed that I couldn't even write and tell you how sorry I was that such a print should have been sent to New York.'

In fact, Ray's apprehensions proved groundless. The world premiere of his maiden film in May 1955 had gone down well at the Museum of Modern Art. Its artistic qualities had triumphed over its undoubted technical imperfections. *Pather Panchali* was now launched on its worldwide odyssey, as we shall discuss in chapter 8. Here, we shall tell only the story of its first theatrical release, in Calcutta in 1955.

Its producer, the West Bengal Government, as per its earlier performance, was in no hurry to release the film. It turned down one offer of distribution before eventually placing *Pather Panchali* in the hands of Aurora Films, which would later part-finance *Aparajito*. A release date of 26 August 1955 was agreed on, with a booking until the end of September. In the meantime, Ray, using his publicity skills, decided to design some large advertisements and have them printed and pasted up entirely on credit. They made a big impact. He also designed a neon sign showing Apu and Durga running together, which was mounted above K. C. Das, the most famous sweet-seller in Calcutta.

Less happily, Ray allowed himself to be persuaded to give the film its Calcutta premiere at the annual meet of the Advertising Club of Calcutta in the ballroom of the Ordnance Club. As one of the organisers later observed, 'The audience was more interested in drinking whisky than in seeing stark reality on the screen.' Ray recalled being 'extremely discouraged' by the reaction. 'There were lots of Englishmen in the crowd – men and women – and they came forward to say how much they liked it. Only English people came forward; nobody else did. There was a little buffet afterwards and people just talked of other things.' In the coffee house later, Subhash Ghosal repeated to him various comments, such as why was the sequence with the waterskaters so long? According to Ray,

> All the criticisms were being related to me in the hope that I would probably make some changes. But I didn't. I just listened to them. My feeling was that the circumstances of the showing were so dismal. The projector was right in the middle of the room and it made a terrific noise and the place had wooden floors, so if people moved their chairs there was a

creaking noise. They were not the right circumstances for the first screening of a film that demanded attention. It needs ideal projection conditions and a quiet audience and rapt attention.

When *Pather Panchali* opened a little later at a Calcutta cinema, it ran poorly to begin with; but within a week or two word got round, and by the end of its booking it was filling the house and people were seeing it three times in a day. Had it not been for the next booking – a south Indian spectacular – the cinema house would have kept *Pather Panchali*. At six o'clock in the morning after the film was taken off at the first cinema, there was a ring at Ray's door. It was the producer of the south Indian film, S. S. Vasan. He had seen *Pather Panchali* and loved it. With tears in his eyes he informed Ray that if he had known about the film in advance, he would have agreed to postpone his own opening. Soon, the film opened again at another cinema, where it ran for a further seven weeks. As Ray's friend R. P. Gupta wrote of *Pather Panchali* in the 1980s, 'All middle-aged and older men and women know the furore ... that followed its first release in Calcutta.'

No sequel to *Pather Panchali* was in Ray's mind when it was completed, as already mentioned. Indeed, he spent some time in mid-1955 searching for a totally different story for his second film. The success of *Pather Panchali* was what finally prompted him to undertake *Aparajito*, and at the same time to resign from his advertising job so as to become a full-time film-maker. Ray began work on the new script in October 1955. Soon after, in February, he mentioned *Aparajito* in a letter to an advertising contact in Bombay as follows: 'I am on the verge of a new venture – a sequel to *Pather Panchali* ... a story with an entirely different texture to it, and a theme of the utmost interest and importance' – that is, Apu's feeling of freedom after the death of his beloved mother. He added: 'I hope to avoid the many shortcomings of PP which resulted partly from my own inexperience and partly from the manner of its making.'

Without doubt, *Aparajito* looks more technically accomplished than *Pather Panchali* (ditto, *The World of Apu* as compared with *Aparajito*). In addition, its narrative flows more like a Hollywood film of its time than the rambling *Pather Panchali*. An American critic, Arlene Croce, wrote somewhat critically of a 'smooth, page-turning professionalism' in *Aparajito*. 'That is a very shrewd comment', Ray remarked later. 'I agree with that to a certain extent. It's a kind of novelistic problem – because I had to tell Apu's story as told in the book. It's a kind of chronicle. I never really went back to that [saga] form any more.'

Nevertheless, there were plenty of problems in its making. Two new actors were required to play the growing Apu: Pinaki Sen Gupta for the Benares and early village scenes, Smaran Ghosal for the adolescent Apu in the village and in Calcutta. Would the audience accept Apu's change in physical appearance? 'It is always a problem with this kind of film', said Ray. 'I kept

Ray on location on the ghats of Benares, 1956, while shooting *Aparajito* with actor Pinaki Sen Gupta

thinking of *Great Expectations* and Pip growing up. We got very fond of the boy Pip, and when at a certain point you suddenly have John Mills appearing as a grown-up Pip, you know it's a different actor and therefore it's a different person altogether. You get a shock, and then you accept it after a certain point.'

The acceptance was made easier by the utter conviction of Karuna Banerji as the mother of all three Apus, who gave unquestionably the finest performance in *Aparajito*. 'I was absolutely overwhelmed by her personality,' she said. 'It all came so naturally to me. Every word, every look, every small movement, the deep attachment towards the alienated son, they all developed within me, as leaves grow outwards on the branch of a tree. Sounds poetic? But believe me, that is exactly how I felt whenever I had a chance to work with Manik [Ray]. Not a single turn of the character that I portrayed was forced, illogical, artificial.'

Shooting in Benares was formidably challenging. Interiors (Harihar's rented rooms) were shot in a Calcutta studio, but exteriors meant working on the ghats, in the lanes and within the temples of the holy city, among its crowds of religious devotees, shifting shadows and diverse sounds. Ray was determined to capture this multitude of sensations through the experiences of Apu, as the opening entry of his diary reveals:

> *1 March 1956* – Set out at 5 a.m. to explore the ghats. Half an hour to sunrise, yet more light than one would have thought, and more activity. The earliest bathers come about 4 a.m., I gather. The pigeons not active yet, but the wrestlers are. Incomparable 'atmosphere'. One just wants to go on absorbing it, being chastened and invigorated by it. The thought of having to work – planning, picking sites and extras, setting up camera and microphone, staging action – is worrying. But here, if anywhere, is a truly *inspiring* setting. It is not enough to say that the ghats are wonderful or exciting or unique. One must get down to analysing the reasons for their uniqueness, their impact. The more you probe, the more is revealed, and

the more you know what to include in your frame and what to leave out.

In the afternoon the same ghats present an utterly different aspect. Clusters of immobile widows make white patches on the greyish ochre of the broad steps. The bustle of ablution is absent. And the light is different, importantly so. The ghats face east. In the morning they get the full frontal light of the sun, and the feeling of movement is heightened by the play of cast shadows. By 4 p.m. the sun is behind the tall buildings whose shadows now reach the opposite bank. Result: a diffused light until sunset perfectly in tune with the subdued nature of the activity.

Morning scenes in the ghat must be shot in the morning and afternoon scenes in the afternoon.

As for the interiors shot in a Calcutta studio, Ray's cameraman Mitra devised a system of 'bounce' lighting, which had never been used in movies. (Ingmar Bergman's cameraman Sven Nykvist later claimed to have invented it, but Nykvist first used it in 1961, five years after *Aparajito* was made.) Instead of direct lighting, with its attendant swarms of moving shadows, shadowless lighting from above was simulated by stretching a sheet of cloth over the set and bouncing studio lights back from it. This matched the actual source of light from the sky in the open courtyards of houses in Benares, particularly those in the area of the city favoured by Bengalis such as Harihar Ray. The 'bounce' system worked so well that no one was aware that the courtyard was faked in a studio, whereas the street outside the courtyard was authentic. 'Besides its truthful character to simulate natural light, bounce lighting has a delicate artistic quality as an additional advantage,' commented Mitra. 'To me, to shoot with nothing but direct lights inside the studios is something like photographing the exteriors only in sunlight, sacrificing all the subtle tints of a rainy day or an overcast sky or dawn or dusk. It is like someone refusing to shoot in the mist or not caring for the poetry present in a cloudy day.'

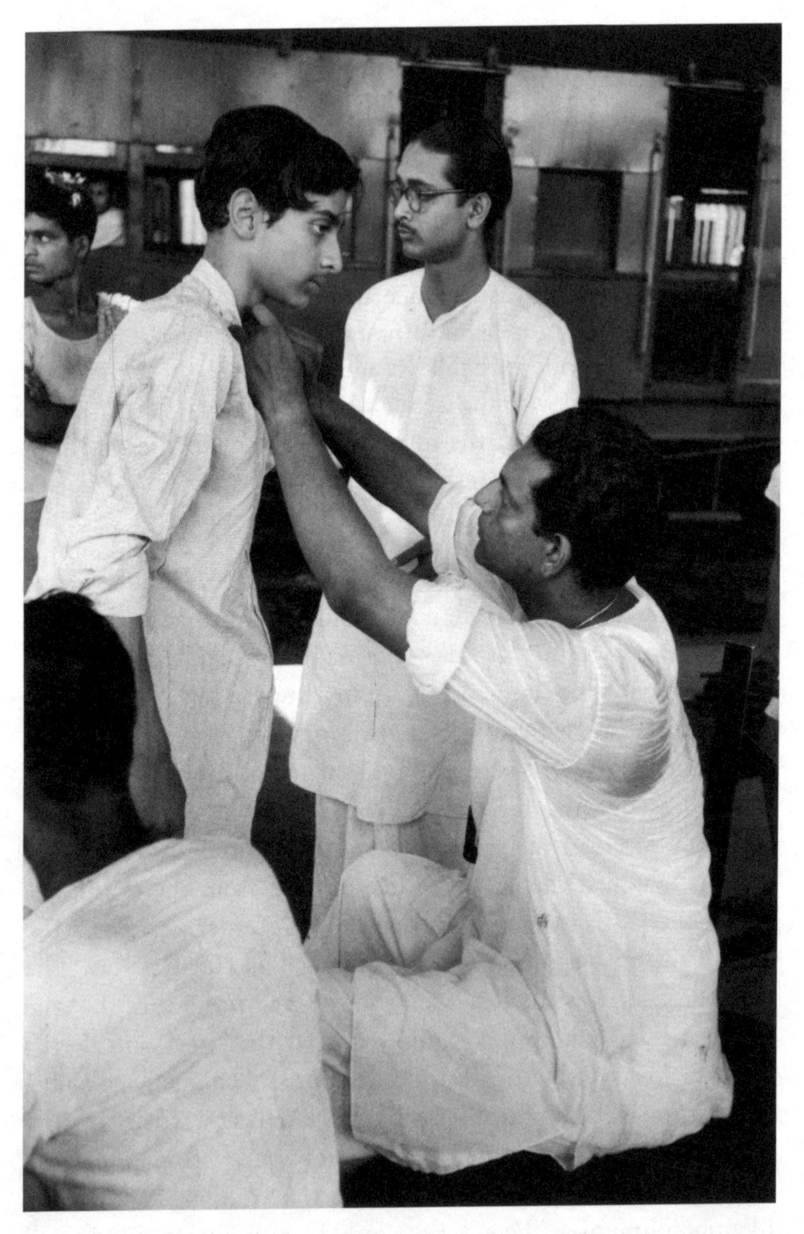

Ray on location at a railway station in Calcutta, 1956, while shooting *Aparajito*, with actor Smaran Ghosal and cameraman Subrata Mitra

In *The World of Apu*, both the acting and the sets reached a consummate pitch of perfection, not to speak of the effortless editing and exquisitely appropriate music by Ravi Shankar. By 1958, not only did Ray have the experience of making four films (*Pather Panchali* and *Aparajito*, of course, and also *Paras Pathar* and *The Music Room/Jalsaghar*, made in 1957–58), he also felt free to depart strongly from Banerji's novel, as explained earlier, which liberated his imagination.

The third film introduced two actors who were to become regulars for Ray. When Soumitra Chatterji, then in his mid-twenties, came to play Apu, having initially approached Ray for the adolescent role in *Aparajito* and been found too old, he identified with almost every aspect of Apu's character, like most of his friends in Calcutta. 'We were to a great extent Apus of our time,' he said later. Sharmila Tagore, who plays Aparna, was only fourteen and still at school. (She is related to the painters Abanindranath and Gaganendranath Tagore, the more orthodox branch of the Tagore family.) She had no acting experience, but she was already a dancer. Ray met Sharmila for the first time – after failing to find Aparna through a newspaper advertisement that attracted over 1,000 replies – when her parents brought her to him and his wife in a frock. 'We made her wear a sari, did her hair differently, and put the sari over her head to suggest a married woman', he said. 'I took a photograph of her and she looked exactly like Aparna.' Though she learnt very quickly, her performance was 'heavily directed'. Ray literally talked her through each shot: 'Now turn your head, now look this way, now look that way, now look down, now come with your lines, pause pause here, and now come with your lines again,' he recalled. As Sharmila herself happily admitted long after she had become a star in Bombay cinema, 'Manikda [Ray] is a tremendous actor.' The boy chosen to play Apu and Aparna's son Kajal, Alok Chakravarti, was only four and a half years old, yet looked ideal for the role. 'I thought I could hardly expect him to give a good performance,' wrote Ray in his autobiography, 'but by now I had acquired some experience in handling children, however small and difficult' – which at one point included giving the boy a sedative to create his wonderfully lifelike scene of awakening from sleep when touched by his father Apu.

Apu's garret, to which he brings his bride, still decked out in her finery, was based on a room in the extreme north of Calcutta that overlooked a series of railway tracks where trains shunted back and forth; but it was constructed by Bansi Chandragupta in the studio, so that Ray and Mitra could have ideal control over the lighting and camerawork. The sights and sounds of railway trains – first heard, then seen, in *Pather Panchali* – are the woof of the Trilogy, drawing it together into an epic work. 'As soon as I decided to do *Aparajito*, I decided to bring back the train; and when I decided to do *Apur Sansar* I had this inspiration,' said Ray. 'I thought I would take away the lyrical element of the train and have the couple living right on the railway track and being bothered by all the whistle and steam and this and that. And then the idea came to my head that after Aparna's death Apu would try to throw himself on the tracks and take his own life. But all that came later.' For Ray, it was essential that his screenplays should evolve organically; he hardly ever began with a framework and fitted his characters into it.

The grand village house of the Apu–Aparna wedding was, by contrast, a real building. Ray and Chandragupta looked at many such decaying zamindari houses in the country before settling on one with a perfect riverine location. 'The river was just right, narrow and winding through mustard flowers', wrote Ray. 'Boats plied and I thought it would be a good idea for Apu and his friend [Pulu] to travel part of the distance by boat. It would make the journey from Calcutta to the village more interesting.' In the event, apart from the exterior of the house and its setting, only its front verandah and its compound were used for shooting, after being repaired; the interior of the house was built in the studio.

While shooting an especially lyrical scene on the river, there was a near-catastrophe. At one end of the boat sat Apu and Pulu; Apu playing his flute and declaiming Tagore's poetry, his friend silently reading Apu's manuscript. At the other end were the old oarsman, the cameraman and his camera, the sound recordist and his equipment, Ray's first assistant Sailen Dutt and Ray himself – making a full load. 'The scene was going well, when suddenly Sailen let out a cry', remembered Ray. 'I said "cut" and turned round to see what Sailen was staring at aghast.' Their boat was on a direct collision course with a huge boat approaching from behind in a narrow part of the river. With the seconds ticking away, Sailen suddenly sprang up, threw himself forward and managed to fend off the other boat with both hands – but at the cost of his foothold. He was flung into the water along with the notebook he had been using to keep continuity. 'It was the narrowest escape from dire disaster that I had ever experienced', Ray recorded in his autobiography. And at the same time a compelling reminder of the unpredictable course of both art and life, epitomised by the Apu Trilogy and its epic making.

4

Working with Ravi Shankar: The Music of the Apu Trilogy

The young Ravi Shankar, who composed most of the music for the Apu Trilogy – a Bengali born in Benares in 1920, the very year in which Satyajit Ray's Apu arrives in the city – first came to prominence in India during the 1940s. By the 1950s, he was regarded as one of the subcontinent's leading classical instrumentalists – both by fellow musicians and music connoisseurs, including Ray. In 1951, while trying to raise interest in his adaptation of the novel *Pather Panchali*, Ray made a series of striking sketches for a documentary film about Shankar: a sort of story-board covering 31 pages of a drawing book, like the one he created in 1952 for *Pather Panchali*. Although the documentary was never made, the sketches were published in 2005 in my book *Satyajit Ray: A Vision of Cinema*. Accompanying the atmospheric wash images are laconic shooting notes – 'truck forward', 'pan away', 'dissolve to' and so on – that give some notion, however incomplete, of what was in Ray's mind.

Shankar is seen with his sitar playing raga *Todi*, a morning raga, at first slowly in the introductory phase known as *alap*, then gradually speeding up; he is still playing as the film ends. Intercut between shots of him and his instrument at various

Sketch by Ray for a documentary film about Ravi Shankar, 1951, which was never made

distances and angles, and the hands of his accompanist playing the tabla, are other, non-musical images. These dwell on nature – drifting clouds, falling leaves, rippling water, lotus flowers flapping, later on trees shaking in a storm – but also include a Rajput miniature painting of the female raga (ragini) *Tori* (such paintings often depict the Indian musical modes), showing a lady with deer near a lotus pond, as well as decorative details from Indian relief sculpture. Clearly, Ray intended that his filmed tribute to Shankar should suggest some essential unity behind the different Indian art forms. It is as if, already, four years before finishing *Pather Panchali*, the budding director had visualised the lyrical, hopeful sequence in the film of the breaking of the monsoon (though ironically raga *Todi* is played in that film by Shankar in the scene following Durga's death, not before the breaking of the monsoon).

In 1992, hearing of the death of Ray on 23 April, Shankar immediately recorded a new composition, 'Farewell, My Friend…', in honour of him. 'In the last couple of days, my heart has been heavy with sorrow, of having lost a friend and such a great, creative genius of our time', he wrote three days after the news reached him. 'The result is this *dhun*' – a north Indian folk melody played in a light classical style – 'I played as a dedication to him. One can hear two melody lines intermingled in this piece. The first is the variation on the theme music which I composed about 40 years ago for his first film – the immortal *Pather Panchali*, the second melody is based on raga *Ahir Bhairav*. … While recording I had flashbacks of some of the wonderful time we spent together and I poured my heart out through my music bidding farewell to my dear friend – Satyajit Ray.'

The mutual respect of Ray and Shankar is evident from the above. Despite an underlying tension and a degree of rivalry between these two powerful but very different creative personalities, and serious differences over the composition of film music, they did indeed remain friendly for decades. Whilst Ray keenly admired Shankar as a virtuoso sitarist and appreciated some of his compositions for stage productions, Shankar felt a reciprocal admiration for many of Ray's films, including some of the music that Ray began composing for his films in 1962. 'He made such sublime films. *Pather Panchali*, *Charulata*, *Kanchenjungha* and *Jalsaghar* will always stand out in my memory', Shankar wrote in 1997, in his autobiography *Raga Mala*; he selected *Pather Panchali* as 'the best film he made, and one of the best I have come across by anyone', for its 'innocent simplicity, straight from the heart without any ego.' In 2009, long after Ray's death, Shankar remarked to an Indian newspaper interviewer: 'Ray understood Indian classical music as much as he knew western classical music. ... Here was a director who would never compromise nor allow me to go overboard. He was confident and rigid about exactly what he required from me or any of his composers. Ray himself was an outstanding composer and music sessions with him are still unforgettable. For the Apu Trilogy, he extracted the true essence of rural Bengal from me musically.'

According to Shankar, the two of them first met in Bombay, not Calcutta, at the end of 1944. 'We became known to each other, though not close friends.' After Shankar gave his first major concert in Calcutta in late 1945, attended by Ray, the two of them began to meet periodically. In the late 1940s and early 50s, when performing in Calcutta, Shankar used to stay in a hotel (the same hotel used by Renoir at this time), which was near Ray's office at Keymer's. 'Many times on his way there, or at lunchtime,' Shankar recalled, 'we would meet for a short while. We became quite friendly. That was about all, until he approached me regarding his first film, *Pather Panchali*.'

This was in late 1954. *Pather Panchali* was still in production when Ray wrote to Ravi Shankar in Delhi and requested him to compose the music for the film. He admired Shankar's music for the ballet *Discovery of India*, composed in 1947; he was also familiar with some of his compositions for films. Shankar immediately agreed. But by the time Ray needed him in very early 1955, the sitarist was in the midst of a concert tour. Postponement of the recording was impossible, given Ray's Museum of Modern Art festival deadline, nor could he contemplate the possibility of replacing the composer. In the event, Shankar managed to combine a very short recording session in Calcutta with a concert. As soon as he arrived in the city, Ray rushed him to the projection room, where he watched half of the film in a roughly edited version; that same afternoon, he composed and recorded the music in a single session ending in the early hours of the following morning.

At the outset, Shankar, with Ray's concurrence, decided not to use any western instruments in *Pather Panchali*. In addition to the sitar, he used three other string instruments: the *dilruba* (*tar-shehnai*), the *bhimraj* (elder brother of the *esraj*) and the *sarod* – plus the *pakhwaj* for percussion.

When the music for the entire trilogy was released on an LP in the late 1970s, Ray described its composition in valuable detail in a sleeve-note, as follows:

> One of the first things that Ravi Shankar did when I met him shortly after his arrival in Calcutta was to hum a line of melody which he said had occurred to him as a possible theme for the film. It was a simple tune with a wistful, pastoral quality which seemed to suit exactly the mood of the film. It went on to become the main theme of *Pather Panchali*.
>
> Since I felt that in the short time that I had it would be too constricting for Ravi Shankar to have to compose to precise, predetermined footages, the method we used was to decide on the mood and instrumental combination for a particular scene, and then provide music well beyond the required length. In addition, we recorded about half-a-dozen three-minute pieces on the sitar in various ragas and tempos. This took care of the risk of running short at the time of fitting the music to the scenes in the cutting room. This is by no means an ideal method, but it has its advantages. For instance, the music that accompanies the ballet of the waterbugs in the film [before

> the arrival of the monsoon] was originally played as one of the several variations on the main theme with no specific scene in mind. In fact, there was no scene of dancing insects in the film at this stage; it grew out of the music in the cutting room.

In *Aparajito*, the same five instruments were used, either solo or in various combinations. But in *The World of Apu*, the musical situation was more complicated, wrote Ray:

> In *Apur Sansar*, Ravi Shankar had to contend with a story that was much more varied in texture than the first two films of the trilogy. It begins in a squalid north Calcutta setting, shifts to the countryside for Apu's wedding, comes back to Calcutta and, after the death of Apu's wife, accompanies the disconsolate hero on his wanderings from seaside to sylvan woods, to the wild and hilly coal-mining areas of Chhota Nagpur, returning finally to the Bengal countryside for the concluding scenes. Five Indian instruments were obviously inadequate to cope with all this, so Ravi Shankar decided to add violins and cellos (even a piano for one particular piece). Also, the usual hectic one-day session was abandoned, and the music was composed and recorded over three days.

On the LP release, the music is divided into the following tracks. For *Pather Panchali*: 'Title Music', 'Variation on the Main Theme', 'Indir's Song', 'The Dance of the Waterbugs', 'Durga Dances in the Rain', 'Life without Durga', 'Sarbajaya's Grief' and 'The Family Leaves the Village'. For *Aparajito*: 'Title Music', 'Harihar Collapses', 'Variation on the Main Theme', 'Apu Grows Up', 'Sarbajaya's Loneliness' and 'Apu Leaves for the City'. For *The World of Apu*: 'Title Music', 'Variation on the Main Theme', 'Apu Comes Home with Bride', 'Life with Aparna', 'Aparna Is No More' and 'Apu's Renunciation'.

In the mid-1980s, when the screenplay of the Apu Trilogy was published in English translation, Ray was somewhat more

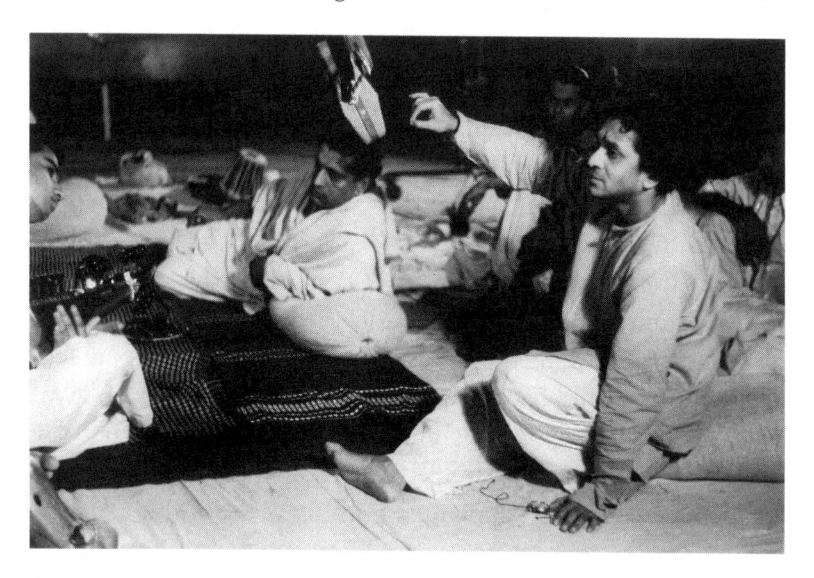

Shankar, with Ray, recording music for *Aparajito* in Calcutta, 1956

precise about its music, specifying the ragas chosen by Shankar. Thus, raga *Desh* was used for the dance of the insects before the monsoon, raga *Todi* after the death of Durga (as already remarked), raga *Patdeep* for Sarbajaya's grief, raga *Jog* with the sudden flight of pigeons after the death of Harihar, raga *Jog* again (in a different orchestration) to suggest Sarbajaya's loneliness in the village, and raga *Lachari Todi* to represent the poignant Apu–Aparna relationship. Ray also noted: 'There is one scene in *Apur Sansar* which is crucial from the point of view of music. It shows Apu's aimless wanderings after Aparna's death, and ends with him throwing away the manuscript of his novel as a gesture of renunciation. The music here, scored for flute and strings, has the noble simplicity of a Vedic hymn.' (This is where a piano is also used.)

One memorable piece in *Pather Panchali* that was *not* composed by Shankar, for lack of time, involved the comic twanging of the single-stringed *ektara*, a folk instrument, that accompanied the wobbling sweet-seller, the children and the dog. 'This caused a problem for Ravi Shankar when he went on a tour of the United States after *Pather Panchali* was released [there] in 1958', noted Ray in his autobiography with a touch of relish. 'At one of his recitals he was asked by a member of the audience to play the candy-man music from the film.' Shankar said he had forgotten how the music went!

Both *Pather Panchali* and *Aparajito*, especially the second film, suffered from Shankar's lack of availability (though not *The World of Apu*). They contained passages of oppressive silence, Ray felt, where music would have helped relieve the slowness. By way of example, 'In *Aparajito*, after Harihar's death, the very first day Sarbajaya and Apu arrive in the village, dusk is falling and there is practically nothing happening, nothing to see – almost nothing to hear – in that long sequence,' Ray said. 'I feel so awkward when I see the scene. But Ravi Shankar hadn't provided any music and I didn't have the confidence to write any.' Still, Ray was grateful to Shankar for the music he did compose, because by 1956 the sitarist was in tremendous demand for concerts, both in India and internationally.

Regrettably, Shankar himself never discussed in any detail his music for the Apu Trilogy, perhaps partly because much of it had been inspired by Ray. He did not say, for instance, what may have influenced his creation of the main theme of *Pather Panchali* before he had even seen the rough cut. This is despite the fact that he thought his music for the trilogy was the best film music he had ever composed. In *Raga Mala*, he noted that Ray wrote to him once to say that it was a pity he could not give more time to his film compositions, and admitted: 'This was true – it was a hit-and-run affair whenever I recorded the score for anyone: I arrived in the city, saw the film, then went to the studio and did the music. I never had time to stay for editing, mixing or improving it. Yet I do believe that whatever came first was always the best, and when I tried to redo a score it was not as good.'

Neither Ray nor Shankar ever said so explicitly, but Ray's 1951 fascinating proposed documentary about him probably failed to materialise because of their disagreement over music for films. After the Apu Trilogy, Shankar did not compose again for Ray, who decided in 1961 that he would prefer to compose his own music rather than wrestling with virtuoso players, such as Shankar, Vilayat Khan (*The Music Room*) and, most difficult of all, Ali Akbar Khan (*The Goddess*), as film composers. Interviewed about Ray's music in 1965, Shankar, while enthusing over the Apu Trilogy and Ray as a director, was notably cool about Ray as a film composer: 'He is competent. He knows exactly what he wants. He has experience in western music, specially the piano.' He added that only Chaplin, among great film directors, had also managed to distinguish himself as a composer.

'We had a slight misunderstanding', wrote Shankar in *Raga Mala*, after Ray's death. 'I was quite hurt because he wrote somewhere that I was unique as a writer of music for ballet and the stage, but he thought film was something else. ... If Satyajit thought he was suitable to do the music for his own films – and people did like it – then he must have been. The director is the boss – and especially when he has the stature Satyajit had earned worldwide.' Wonderfully apt though Shankar's music for the Apu Trilogy was, Ray came to feel that he himself was the more gifted film composer – rightly in the view of many musicians – especially as his knowledge of and feeling for western music was undoubtedly far superior to Shankar's. Such western elements were crucial for his later, more urban films, as compared to the village-inspired Apu Trilogy. 'The average educated middle-class Bengali may not be a sahib,' said Ray in 1980, 'but his consciousness is cosmopolitan, influenced by western modes and trends. To reflect that musically you have to blend – to do all kinds of experiments. Mix the sitar with the alto and the trumpet and so on ... It's a tricky matter, but the challenge cannot be shirked.' Ray's complex, varied and subtle scores composed over three decades, from *Kanchenjungha* in 1962 to *The Stranger* in 1991, including his own highly popular songs for *The Adventures of Goopy and Bagha* – amply demonstrate this truth.

5

Pather Panchali: Critique

Some two decades after the first release of *Pather Panchali*, Akira Kurosawa said of it:

> I can never forget the excitement in my mind after seeing it. I have had several more opportunities to see the film since then and each time I feel more overwhelmed. It is the kind of cinema that flows with the serenity and nobility of a big river.
>
> People are born, live out their lives, and then accept their deaths. Without the least effort and without any sudden jerks, Ray paints his picture, but its effect on the audience is to stir up deep passions. How does he achieve this? There is nothing irrelevant or haphazard in his cinematographic technique. In that lies the secret of its excellence.

Ray's film-making is the art that conceals art; by the greatest economy of means he creates films that are among the most life-like in the history of cinema. Effortlessness is a hallmark of all his best work. As he said – and always strove for on screen – 'The best technique is the one that's not noticeable.'

This means that his films resist thoroughgoing analysis. Even to describe the plot or story of *Pather Panchali* is a challenge, with or without the aid of the published screenplay. There are some turning points, of course, such as the birth of Apu, his first day at school, the death of Indir, the arrival of the monsoon, the death of Durga, the return of Harihar, the departure from the village. But the essence of the film lies in the ebb and flow of its human relationships and in its everyday details and cannot be reduced to a tale of events. For how can one narrate the entire experience of childhood – the main subject of *Pather Panchali*? Moreover, childhood that is seen not only from the point of view of Apu, but also from those of his sister and his two parents.

The film critic Robin Wood accurately acknowledged this in his study of the Apu Trilogy when he wrote:

> In the West, we are conditioned primarily either by the classic American cinema with its taut narrative structures in which, when a scene has made its point, we are carried swiftly on to the next, or by the European 'art' cinema with its tendency to intellectual thematic structures. We may feel, with Ray, that we have already got the point when we are in fact continuing to miss it, for 'the point' may not be an extractable thematic or narrative issue but the total experience a character is undergoing.

The same idea was encapsulated by Ray's father, the nonsense-verse writer and illustrator Sukumar Ray, in an essay on Rabindranath Tagore: 'Where poetry is coextensive with life itself, where art ceases to be the mere expression of imaginative impulse, it is futile to attempt a comprehensive analysis.' By the standards of most directors, not very much happens in the majority of Ray's films – as John Huston sensed in 1954 when he saw some rough cut of *Pather Panchali* – and yet each film seems to embody the way of life of a section of Bengali society.

Taken together, as with Kurosawa's films and Japanese society but markedly more so, Ray's films describe a whole culture.

Pather Panchali, *Aparajito* and *The World of Apu* are very different in their dominant moods and in the rewards they offer the viewer. They reflect the consciousness of Apu as it evolves from innocence, and this gives them a coherence that it is tempting to call musical. As a whole, the trilogy is reminiscent of the development of a raga, the basic classical Indian melodic form, in which the music flows, sometimes meandering, through its prescribed phases towards its emotional catharsis – from Apu's introduction into the world to his reunion with his small abandoned son in the finale of *The World of Apu*. A raga traditionally has three sections: First, the *alap*, 'the very slow introductory movement of a raga, featuring the gradual and meditative unfolding of its structure, theme and *rasa* [emotion]... considered the highest form in Indian music... [with] no measured time cycle', in the words of Ravi Shankar. Secondly, the more complex *jor*, which is still a solo exposition but which introduces a rhythmic pulse and has a gradually increasing tempo. Finally, the *jhala*, when the strings of the instrumentalist are joined by the beat of the tabla in a fixed rhythmic cycle that nevertheless allows for ample improvisation, and the tempo increases to a climax at the end. *Pather Panchali* may be compared to the *alap*, *Aparajito* to the *jor*, and *The World of Apu* to the *jhala* phases of a raga.

At the beginning of *Pather Panchali*, Apu does not, of course, exist: for some considerable time into the film, the family consists of Harihar, Sarbajaya, little Durga and Indir. We first see Apu as a baby, rocked by the ancient Indir Thakrun, but we first meet him as an eye. He is by then about six. On Sarbajaya's instructions, Durga wakes up Apu for his first day at school by gently prising open his reluctant eyelid. He is a skinny, shy little boy with a ravenous curiosity, and frequently a hunger for food too – but his mother can seldom provide what she would like to give him. No matter: he and his sister live in their own worlds,

Pather Panchali: little Durga; Indir Thakrun and Durga

sometimes separate, sometimes together. Secretly they share a pickle made with oil stolen from their mother; trail behind the itinerant sweet-seller whose wares they cannot afford; listen to Auntie Indir telling them ghost stories at night; marvel at the peep-show of the 'bioscopewallah' displaying images of faraway places; and huddle together in a monsoon downpour, as the village seasons change. One day, feeling annoyed with each other, they run across the fields around the village and out of their familiar world. There, in the unknown, among the feathery white *kash* grasses, they become friends again and have their first tingling encounter with a railway train belching black smoke. On their way back home through the forest, leading the family cow and giggling and tickling each other, they meet something even more incomprehensible – Death. Indir, their 'auntie', rejected by Sarbajaya, has come into the forest to die. Sometime later, in the monsoon, Durga too dies from a fever brought on by the rain, during a savage overnight thunderstorm. Without being told, Apu begins to understand death for himself. Harihar is away at the time, trying every possible avenue to make some money; on his return he is compelled to confront his full failure as a husband and as a man. He decides to take Sarbajaya and Apu to Benares, where he will earn a living by reading aloud the scriptures. The last image in the film is of the three of them trundling slowly away from Nishchindipur in an ox cart.

Let us now consider some of the striking sequences from *Pather Panchali*, and from the other two films of the trilogy in the following two chapters, so as to have a clearer picture of Ray's *mise-en-scène*. They have been chosen to reveal, I hope, how Ray builds up Apu's world and allows us to enter his thoughts as they grow in maturity with age and experience.

Apu's first day at school, early in the film, is a good place to begin. Banerji, the writer of *Pather Panchali*, devoted about ten pages of his novel to the school of the grocer–schoolmaster, for whom caning is a frequent substitute for teaching. Ray distilled these pages into a mere four minutes, in which he packs a microcosm of human behaviour, which teeters on the edge of comedy and cruelty, rather like the novels and stories of the south Indian writer R. K. Narayan. The schoolmaster's cane, for example, is prominently stuck, for ease of use, in his grocer's tub of salt.

Although little happens in this school scene, there is a lot to look at and listen to. In a short span we see the school from multiple perspectives: those of the tubby, pop-eyed grocer–schoolmaster and the pupil Apu, but also those of a girl customer, a leathery-faced village elder come to sponge off the grocer, and the rest of the boys in the class who are of various ages and levels of mischief. All the while that the multi-tasking schoolmaster is giving the boys a sonorous dictation of poetic phrases from a text retelling the story of the epic *Ramayana*, he is also measuring out goods and selling them to his customers, gossiping with his visitor, rebuking and chastising his pupils, scratching his back with the cane and loudly yawning. The innocent Apu – new to this quotidian, slapstick spectacle – at first grins spontaneously, abruptly becomes serious after a scolding, and is finally afraid for his own skin after being forced to watch the caning of an older boy caught playing noughts and crosses on his slate. So sharp is the 'thwack' that it can be heard across the quiet village pond. All this is teaching of a kind – but an education more in the ways of the world than in the pursuit of knowledge (though the schoolmaster is clearly not a total philistine; he has some feeling for the grand language he is dictating from memory). When Apu next goes to school, in *Aparajito*, and proves to be an earnest pupil, we know that he is aware of the ignominious fate he has escaped at the hands of the grocer–schoolmaster.

An extract from the script gives some idea of Ray's dramatic skill and the scene's humour:

Schoolmaster: (*dictating*) 'Deep in the heart of Janasthan... Deep in the heart of Janasthan!' (*He glares at the boys.*) Harey! Harey! What are up to now? How many more times must you moisten your duster? Eh? Sit down! 'Deep in the heart of Janasthan ...' Well, Puti, what do you want?

Girl customer: One paisa worth of puffed rice.

Schoolmaster: Puffed rice? A paisa worth? Hand over the money then. ... 'the lordly mount Prasraban stands ... the lordly mount Prasraban stands! Its godlike summit ... Its godlike summit ...' (*Puti collects her puffed rice. The schoolmaster yawns.*) '... wears as a crown ... ever-moving clouds ... which ceaseless gales ... which ceaseless gales ...'

(*A village elder, as he approaches the shop/school, starts a loud conversation with the grocer/schoolmaster, who pretends to listen, while continuing to glare at the class.*)

Village elder: How are you, Prasanna?

Schoolmaster: '... which ceaseless gales ...' Oh welcome, welcome, Mr Majumdar!

Village elder: (*stepping past a hole in the road*) Dear me, it's a trap to kill people!

Schoolmaster: '... urge down ... the paths of the air ...'

Village elder: (*to a man sunning himself outside the shop*) Namaskar, Mr Chatterji. Everything alright with you?

Schoolmaster: '... the paths of the air.' Welcome, welcome!

Village elder: You've netted a fine catch, eh? How many pupils now?

Schoolmaster: (*smiles*) The new boy makes nine.

Village elder: Good heavens! The nine gems!

Schoolmaster: (*glaring at the boys*) What's that? Apurba! Why are you grinning? –

Village elder: (*chatting to the man outside the shop*) Take my grandson, just eight years old ...

Schoolmaster: (*addressing Apu*) – Is this a playhouse? (*He scratches his back with his cane.*)

Pather Panchali: Apu is made ready for his first day at school by Sarbajaya and Durga; the grocer–schoolmaster Prasanna

Village elder:	(*looking at Apu*) Go on like that and you'll end up behind a plough. (*Apu's grin vanishes.*)
Schoolmaster:	(*smiling at his visitor*) Well, well. What were you saying, Mr Majumdar? ...
Village elder:	Tell me, have you seen a good *jatra* lately?

He goes on to extol extravagantly a travelling theatre troupe he is about to book for the village; helps himself to some free hair oil from the shop; then leans confidentially towards the schoolmaster and mutters (out of the boys' earshot) that he will not be asking him for a subscription this year, given his helpfulness in other ways.

When Apu returns home with his father from his first day at school, Sarbajaya is cooking. Durga is out of sight but she calls Apu. Conspiratorially she tells him to fetch her secret stock of mustard oil from the top of some shelves inside the house. Meanwhile, Indir Thakrun, by showing off her tattered shawl to Harihar, induces him to promise her a new one. His offer is overheard by a resentful Sarbajaya. When Harihar then asks for cinders for his tobacco pipe, she gives them reluctantly and launches into a list of all the things he is failing to do for his immediate family, without mentioning Indir's shawl directly. 'Have you taken a look at the state of the house, what the children are eating, what clothes they are wearing?' she asks.

Apu can no doubt hear all this, but he is intent on reaching the high shelf. His parents' preoccupation will help him to do this unnoticed. As Sarbajaya carries on, we see Apu approach the shelf and then, in an interesting shot from *behind* the shelf, pick up the coconut shell of oil. Exactly the same pair of shots will be repeated at the end of the film to powerful effect, as Apu clears the shelf before departure and discovers the necklace his dead sister once stole from the neighbours – a visual repetition that thereby recalls the brother and sister's earlier intimacy.

Crouched in their corner, the children share the tamarind paste Durga has made. Apu is tasting its strong sourness for the first time. He lets slip the sound of a grimace. Durga slaps him lightly: 'Idiot! Mother will hear you.' After this brother and sister share their delicious secret in silence, in several shining close-ups. But suddenly Durga is on to something new; her alert hearing has caught the faint tinkle of bells. The sweet-seller has arrived! Obviously she knows him from past visits. Tamarind paste and parents forgotten, the two children jump up and go to a gap in the wall of their house. Outside, the jovial sweet-seller pauses enquiringly. Durga sends Apu running off to beg money from their father who is an easier touch than their mother. But Sarbajaya, still in the kitchen, detects what is going on and calls out to the indulgent Harihar not to give any coins.

Disappointed, the children run out after the sweet-seller; they know he is heading for their neighbour Sejbou's house. A village dog trots out after them, sensing food. As the small procession passes along, it is reflected upside down in the waters of a village pond lightly ruffled by a breeze. The plonking, rustic sound of the one-stringed *ektara*, accompanied by sitar, imparts a perfect rhythm to the odd little group: the wobbling sweet-seller yoked to his swaying, bobbing pots, hungrily pursued by the children and their canine companion. This brief wordless interlude of lyrical happiness belongs uniquely to the cinema; it is the kind of peak in Ray's work that prompted Kurosawa to conclude: 'Not to have seen the cinema of Ray means existing in the world without seeing the sun or the moon.'

In these few scenes, Ray conveys to us the inter-relationships of Harihar's family members with pinpoint clarity. Simultaneously, we come to feel how each parent sees Apu and Durga, how each child sees their mother and father and each other, and how Ray sees them all. *Pather Panchali* is a film about unsophisticated people shot through with sophistication, and without a trace of condescension or inflated sentiment.

Later in the film, there is an especially rich sequence of contrasting incidents of a variety that gives *Pather Panchali* its universal reputation for vivacity and charm. In barest outline, Apu

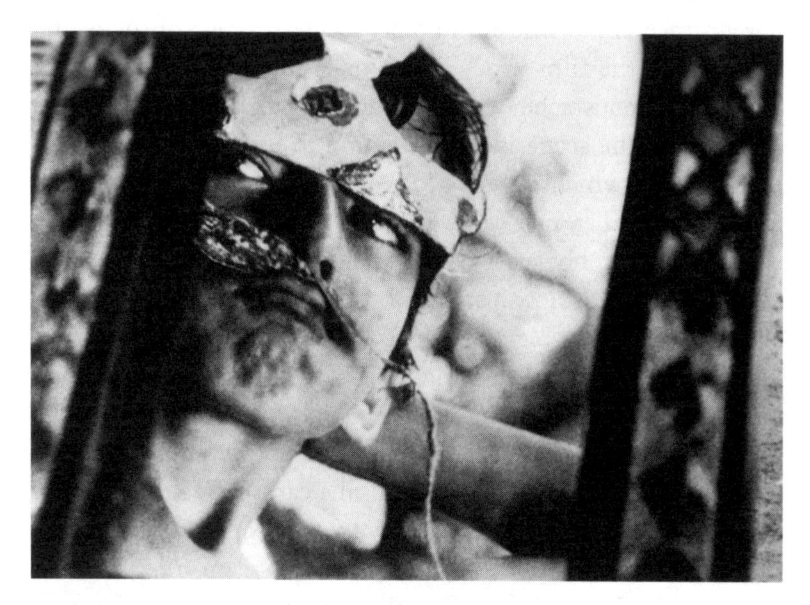

Pather Panchali: Durga; Apu dresses up as a prince

attends a village *jatra* (theatre) performance and is entranced by the actors; at home he dresses up as a prince using Durga's precious tinsel without her permission; they fight and are broken up by Sarbajaya; Durga runs off into the fields in search of the family cow, chased by Apu; meanwhile Indir, seriously ill, returns to the house but is ruthlessly rejected by Sarbajaya; wandering in the fields, Apu and Durga see a railway train; on their way back with the cow they find Indir on the point of death; Indir's body is taken away for cremation.

To the eyes of the viewer, or at least the western viewer who does not follow the language and the mythological story of the villainous Serpent King, his daughter and her noble husband, the pantomime histrionics of the theatre troupe are delightfully incongruous, if a shade too lengthy. But to the enthralled eyes of Apu, standing in the front row of the audience, they appear as real as the dramas of his own life, enacted in the 'playhouse' of his school, at home and among the neighbours. In Banerji's novel, Apu befriends one of the impoverished boy actors playing a prince and brings him home, where the two of them sing together. In the film, Apu, alone, makes himself a tinsel crown and a stage moustache (which he fails to attach to his upper lip). Either way, the scene is an intimation to us of Apu's power of imagination, which in years to come will lead to his desire to become a novelist, in *The World of Apu*.

With Durga, however, in the scenes that follow, Apu is still very much the callow younger brother to her knowledgeable elder sister. She is big enough to catch him and slap him for his theft of her tinsel, leaving him with eyes full of tears and reproach and her stinging rebuke: 'Ass! All dressed up like a prince!' (She understands, as Apu does not yet, that they are paupers who will never be princes.) She can run faster than him through the fields. She knows how to chew sugarcane properly. Her alert ears and eyes spot the monstrous steam train, puffing black smoke, before his do. Yet there are many things that neither child yet grasps, for example, where the train is going and what happens when a person dies. And it is Apu, not Durga, who races the train, climbs the railway embankment, and is seen – now without his crown – by the camera from the other side of the tracks, through gaps in the passing train wheels, excitedly watching the train disappear into the distance. Again, it is a hint of his coming career as a regular train traveller and future student of science. Durga, who on her sickbed will later wistfully mention the train to Apu and look forward to seeing another train with him, is destined never again to set eyes on one.

Appropriately, it is Durga too who first spots their dying auntie squatting in the bamboo grove. As Apu looks on in anticipation, an affectionate Durga tries to wake up the old woman by shaking her – as once we saw her wake up her young brother on the morning of his first day at school by opening his sleeping eye with her fingers. But instead of the old aunt awaking, her body crashes to the ground. No description in words could capture the mingling of beauty, horror and mystery in this scene. The strange, subdued atmosphere is obliquely intensified by three details: the faintly sinister creaking of the tall bamboos, the disarranged wisps of Durga's hair outlined against the sky, and the glinting metal water pot of old Indir that Durga accidentally kicks down the slope into a ditch as she runs away. We have seen this pot many times before, when its owner was alive; now she will never again have need of it or the life-giving water she so recently begged from a reluctant Sarbajaya.

Towards the end of the film, on a morning after Durga's death, there is another sequence that epitomises the many-stranded texture of *Pather Panchali* – this time with overt emotion. It begins with Apu silently cleaning his teeth near the pond, an unfamiliar faraway look in his eyes. Sarbajaya, her hair dishevelled and her sari crumpled, draws water from the village well. Apu goes into the monsoon-devastated house, roughly combs his hair and wraps his shawl around him – actions that a doting sister and mother used to perform. He picks up an empty oil bottle and is about to set off for the grocer's store when he looks up at

Pather Panchali: Sarbajaya rejects Indir

the sky and decides to fetch an umbrella; now he has to think of that too.

The verandah where the long-deceased Indir used to cook, has somehow escaped the storm. Sarbajaya finds herself cooking there. She is dead to the world, and when a neighbour comes bringing food, she does not even notice her presence. It takes the voice of her husband calling for his children to make her stir. We know that Harihar has returned, oblivious of the disaster to his family. Characteristically, both for him and for Ray's sense of drama, he is in good spirits, despite the damage to his house that he cannot avoid seeing all around him. As Sarbajaya mutely fetches him a seat, towel and water from inside and turns to go, Harihar stops her. He wants to show her the presents he has managed to bring. The third item, a sari for Durga which he presses her to admire, is too much for Sarbajaya. To Harihar's great surprise she breaks out in unstoppable weeping, expressed by the high notes of the *tarshehnai* described earlier. When Harihar at last grasps that he has lost his daughter, he collapses over his wife's body.

Another director might have chosen to end the agonising scene there. Ray, instead, returns us to Apu, a sad little figure standing behind the house holding the bottle of oil, which is now full. Without expression he absorbs the sound of his father's sobs. This wordless shot, repeated like this, punctuates the experience of his sister's death, creating a satisfying sense of Apu's emerging knowledge of the world, and acts as a subtle pointer to the growing dominance of Apu as the trilogy progresses.

By the time we reach the very end, the hitherto passive Apu is ready to take his first major decision in life. When he finds the necklace hidden in a coconut shell on a high shelf, in the novel he is described by Banerji as 'lost in thought'. In the film – to the accompaniment of an urgent drumming on the soundtrack – we see Apu quickly pick up the dusty necklace from the floor, glance towards the door to see if either of his parents or any of

Pather Panchali: Harihar collapses over Sarbajaya; village elders visit Harihar

the visiting neighbours or village elders has seen it, run out of the house through a gap in the wall and, with barely a pause, hurl the evidence into the pond. As the necklace plops into the water, briefly disturbing the pondweed, there is a reaction shot, a close-up, of Apu's face with an inscrutable expression, which lasts a few moments. Then the film moves on to its inexorable conclusion. When I once asked Ray how he would describe Apu's state of mind here in the film, he replied: 'It's very complicated. He certainly doesn't want anyone else to know.' But is he hiding the knowledge from himself too, I persisted. 'Yes. Because obviously he knows that his sister had actually stolen it. He probably thinks it's a shame that she did it. But then... I cannot describe the state of mind really – it's much too complicated. Essentially cinematic.'

'I have a feeling that the really crucial moments in a film should be wordless,' Ray said on another occasion, while discussing the wordless ending of his *Charulata*. If one thinks of *Pather Panchali*, this dictum is true. When a scene could have been played out conventionally through dialogue, Ray preferred to find a telling countenance, gesture, movement or sound to express the emotions more dramatically. The first awakening of Apu by Durga; the sweet-seller's procession; Indir's rejection by Sarbajaya; the children's first sight of the train; the death of Indir; the monsoon downpour in which Durga dances; the breakdown of Sarbajaya and Harihar; Apu's disposal of the necklace – they are all made the more memorable for being wordless. What makes *Pather Panchali* a great film is, finally, that it speaks to us – whether we are Indians, Europeans, Americans, Japanese or whoever – not primarily through its plot, dialogue or ideas, but through its apparently inevitable current of ineffable images.

6

Aparajito: Critique

Of the three films in the Apu Trilogy, *Aparajito* tends to be the least admired – both in India and in the West, despite its winning the top prize at the Venice Film Festival in 1957. When it was first released in Calcutta the year before this award, it was a box-office failure, unlike *Pather Panchali* and *The World of Apu*. However, *Aparajito* was the most admired of the trilogy by Ray's fellow Bengali directors Ritwik Ghatak and Mrinal Sen. Sen explained why in the Calcutta *Statesman* in the 1980s:

> In *Aparajito*, Ray's unorthodox approach to the analysis and unfolding of the relationship between a mother and her only son growing into adulthood is, indeed, a revelation. The focus is on the slow but inevitable disintegration of a seemingly unalterable relationship, with constant stresses and strains acting within, and the eventual discovery of the son's new moorings in a metropolitan setting. The entire process, as I watch the film, has its ups and downs, its complexities, its inexorabilities which are ruthless and yet so much an integral part of us and our time.... Honestly, from none of Ray's other films did

I get so much of a punch as I got from *Aparajito* on my first viewing, and continue to get even now.

In my own view, the evocation of the sacred city of Benares – Apu's new home after leaving Nishchindipur – in the first section of *Aparajito* (about a third of the film) easily matches in richness and variety the evocations of Apu's village and nature in *Pather Panchali* and of his Calcutta environment and its urban grime in *The World of Apu*. If the remaining two-thirds of *Aparajito* is sometimes a less rich experience, notably in its Calcutta scenes, the viewer is compensated by the finest performance of any actor in the Apu Trilogy – not excluding Chunibala Devi as Indir in *Pather Panchali* or Soumitra Chatterji as Apu in *The World of Apu*: that of Karuna Banerji as Sarbajaya. From her first appearance in a Benares courtyard to her death in the village of Mansapota at the end of *Aparajito*, she unifies it with her total conviction as Apu's mother – even more than with her performance in *Pather Panchali*.

Certainly, *Aparajito* is neither as lyrical as *Pather Panchali*, nor as moving as *The World of Apu*, but its characterisation is the deepest in the three films, by virtue of Sarbajaya and her relationship with her son. Although one may have little sympathy with her comparatively narrow and passive outlook on life, one cannot avoid becoming emotionally entangled in the poignancy of her predicament. For Apu to be free to grow and realise his talents, Sarbajaya must be abandoned and die: this profound truth is what gripped Satyajit Ray in the novel *Aparajito*, as we know. An unflinching honesty pervades the film, also seen in *Pather Panchali* (for instance, in Sarbajaya's rejection of Indir Thakrun) and *The World of Apu* (for example, Apu's rejection of his infant son), yet in neither of those films is this sustained throughout the film, as it is throughout *Aparajito*.

Before Sarbajaya and Apu make their appearance, the film opens with a sort of timeless documentary montage of intriguing images and a babel of sounds, where barely a word is articulated in the first four or five minutes, which establishes the unique atmosphere of the bathing ghats in Benares. To quote the published screenplay:

> A train rumbles across a bridge. Through the window, steel girders flash past, revealing brief glimpses of a wide river, the holy Ganges.
>
> TITLE: Varanasi [Benares]. Year 1327 (Bengali calendar) [1920].
>
> Dawn over the city of Varanasi. Near the ghat, an old man stands on a flat roof, scattering grain. A flock of pigeons flutter over the roofs of buildings, the air reverberating with the noise of their wings. There are pigeons everywhere, on the carved temple walls, on the thatch covering of sunshades on the ghat steps, over the water at the edge of the river. They come flapping their wings at the call of the old man, and settle down on the roof where he stands. There are people everywhere too. An old widow sits praying under a torn sunshade. Men, women and children bathe in the river. The *kathak thakurs* recite holy verses, surrounded by devotees. The temple bells ring in the morning air. In the river, boats lie moored in the shallows. Fishing nets rest against the walls of the ghat.
>
> Harihar carries the holy water of the river in a little brass pot, up the steps of the ghat. He stops to collect his glasses from another *kathak* who sits under a neighbouring sunshade on the steps, smears some *sindur* [vermilion] on his forehead from the coconut shell that the *kathak* offers him, then goes up the steps again. He enters one of the narrow meandering lanes of the city, sprinkling holy water on the deities placed on either side of the lane. He turns into a narrower lane and enters a door on the right. It is an old-fashioned brick house. The rooms, in two storeys, are built around a small courtyard. The Rays live on the ground floor. Sarbajaya is washing the courtyard, sweeping the water away with a broom. Harihar hangs his shawl on the clothes-line.

Aparajito: Apu in Benares

The parents have a conversation, partly about their absent son, which prepares us for the enchanting entry of Apu, now played by a new boy, Pinaki Sen Gupta, rather than Subir Banerji of the first film. Like Apu's playful first appearance as an eye in the hole of a blanket in *Pather Panchali*, Apu in *Aparajito* is first seen only in part: as a sensitive little face peering around the corner of a wall painted with a dog. Behind the corner of another wall decorated with a rabbit, another boy is hiding. Apu and a group of friends are chasing each other through the lanes, nooks and corners in the area around his house. Often there is so little space to move that the boys have to squeeze past obstacles – first one boy, then another, is seen ducking under the stomach of a ruminating cow.

It is Apu who now personalises the ghats for us after the, as it were, pigeon's-eye view in the film's opening sequence. Alone (unlike in the novel), he wanders by the riverside with a small paper windmill in his hands, observing a particular ghat's goings-on curiously without fully understanding what he sees. First, he gazes at his father seated on some steps surrounded by women, mainly widows in white, as Harihar serenely interprets religious texts from the Sanskrit into Bengali in front of a collection plate with some coins in it. Then he skips away along the ghat, the sound of his father's declamation fading away on the soundtrack, until he reaches the next *kathak* who – like a tour guide in a cathedral – has *his* group of devoted listeners. Apu is not interested, but the film pauses to give us time to absorb the second reciter's very different, melodramatic, 'masala' story-telling (about the love of Radha and Krishna): as different from Harihar's reading as Bollywood films are from Ray films. Meanwhile, Apu, still clutching his windmill, has climbed onto the deck of an empty moored boat. From there he spots something interesting further along the ghat and runs towards it. On one of the many platforms by the river's edge there is an alfresco gymnasium. A muscular man is exercising with a heavy club. In a friendly way he offers Apu a go, but the small boy shyly refuses.

Instead he watches, fascinated by the rhythm of the swing and the man's strange accompanying grunt. As the scene fades into dusk over the whole ghat seen from the river, we understand both the ten-year-old Apu's dawning new horizons and his subliminal rejection of both the priestly and the manual way of life.

The sequence of scenes in Benares that describe the illness and death of Harihar demonstrates Ray's unobtrusive use of contrasts of all kinds to enrich a film and make it mysterious and poetic. First, we see Sarbajaya and Apu visiting the chief shrine of the temple-ridden city, the Viswanath Temple, where they experience the *arati*, the cacophonous evening ritual of chanting and bell-ringing through a haze of incense. The spectacle mesmerises Sarbajaya, but not her son. Back in their ground-floor rooms, she decorates them with a hundred little points of light, the burning wicks that a pious Hindu lights to celebrate the autumn festival of Dusserah (Durga Puja in Bengal).

Into this luminous setting comes Harihar carrying some shopping, and obviously in a weak condition. He has to lie down. Outside the window next to him, a series of fireworks explode in a burst of light and noise that is slightly menacing. Then Apu bursts in holding a large sparkler, eager to show it to his mother. His face falls. Sarbajaya tells him to sit with his father. A little hesitantly Apu answers his father's affectionate questioning. Harihar's feverish mind has taken a nostalgic turn; he asks Apu if the Benares fireworks are as good as the ones in Nishchindipur, their ancestral village. Probably to please his father, Apu says they are not. But what he really wants is to get back to his friends outside. His father gently releases him. Instead, he discusses with Sarbajaya a better dwelling that he may have found for them. Outside, as the night is filled with sparks and bangs, Apu is humming his own version of the tune he has picked up earlier from their upstairs neighbour, the somewhat sleazy bachelor Nanda Babu, a tabla player. The original is a *thumri*, a romantic song with a slightly disreputable air; Apu, with the ingenuousness of a child, has drained

Aparajito: Harihar collapses at the ghat

it of its erotic quality. Nothing is spelt out here, but in this ditty lingers the faint suggestion that we have not heard the last of Nanda Babu.

The following morning, despite Sarbajaya's protest, Harihar goes out to the ghats to earn money by recitation. After bathing in the river, he begins to climb the steps, just as he did at the beginning of the film. (Ray more or less repeats the shots.) But this time Harihar forgets to collect his glasses and has to be reminded by his fellow *kathak* seated by the river, who calls out to him and holds out the glasses. Hearing the call, Harihar looks momentarily confused and puts his right hand up to feel if he is wearing his glasses. 'A small action – which speaks volumes', aptly comments the film writer Ujjal Chakraborty. No one who wears glasses constantly can be unaware of their absence, unless he is fatigued, ill or mentally preoccupied. The steep climb up the steps now proves to be too much for Harihar; near the top he collapses dramatically and has to be helped home. He is plainly dying. Whilst a doctor, Sarbajaya and a neighbouring couple gather round him, the bulky figure of Nanda Babu loiters outside the bars of the sickroom's window. 'I hope he hasn't hurt himself,' he says disingenuously. Immediately after this sombre composition we see Apu absorbed in watching a bulging leather water bag as it is drawn from a well by bullocks. Pressure forces the water to come spurting out through numerous small ruptures. One thinks, without being asked to, of the life that is leaking out of Apu's father. We see Harihar lying motionless.

The shot that follows is one of the most expressive of the many examples in Ray's work of 'a dewdrop which reflects in its convexity the whole universe around it' (an idea he found in Tagore's poetry; also found, of course, in western poets such as William Blake and W. B. Yeats). It begins with a close-up of two pathetic kittens – reminiscent of Durga's kittens in the village – playing with a wooden toy common in Benares on the steps leading upstairs from Harihar's ground-floor rooms. From the top of the frame now appear two feet clad in shiny new pumps – obviously Nanda Babu's. One of the pumps prods one of the skinny little

Aparajito: Apu and Nanda Babu

creatures, not so much because it is in the way, but out of a casual cruelty typical of its owner. That is all. In a sense, nothing of any significance has happened, and yet Sarbajaya's defencelessness has been crystallised; we now expect the worst. Again Nanda Babu appears behind the barred window, but this time no one is there, except for the prone motionless figure of Harihar.

Ray's handling of what happens next – Nanda Babu's pass at Sarbajaya – is charged with meaning for an Indian. She is in the kitchen where outsiders do not normally go and where contact with others while cooking is taboo. As she hears the sound of the pumps approaching she draws her sari over her head in a timeless gesture of Indian womanhood. His face unseen, Nanda Babu slips off his pumps, crosses the threshold, and takes a few steps, his fingers splayed out and trembling with sexual excitement. '*Bouthan*,' he says in a low voice, 'are you making *pan*?' – the spicy betel-nut preparation whose connotations range from the devotional to the frankly disreputable, but which are always associated with intimacy. 'It is a nucleus for hospitality,' wrote E. M. Forster in his celebration 'Pan', 'and much furtive intercourse takes place under its little shield.' Sarbajaya, with blind instinct, threatens Nanda Babu with a kitchen blade, and he beats a hasty retreat.

From here on, the sequence is unrelievedly bleak. At dawn, Harihar just manages to get the words 'Ganges water' past his lips, and his wife knows he is almost gone. Apu walks quickly down to the river's edge to fetch it and returns in the nick of time. As Harihar's soul departs his body, a huge flock of pigeons takes flight and wheels dramatically against the dawn sky, above the rooftops of Benares, accompanied by the falling notes of a flute playing a melody based on raga *Jog*. It will be heard again when Sarbajaya herself begins to die, and in *The World of Apu* when Apu is mentally dead. Ray recalled that at the Venice Film Festival, this particular moment in *Aparajito* brought forth 'a spontaneous burst of applause' from the capacity audience. Besides its obvious religious symbolism – especially appropriate

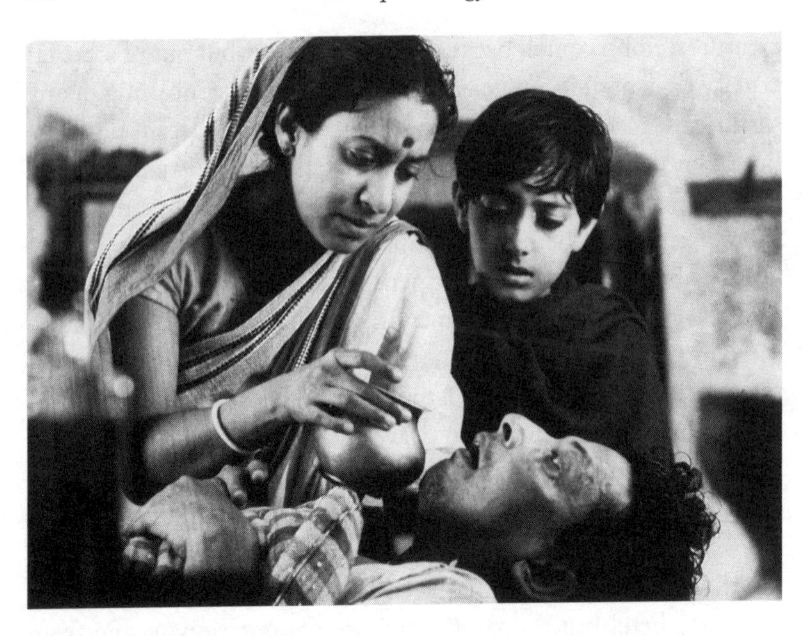

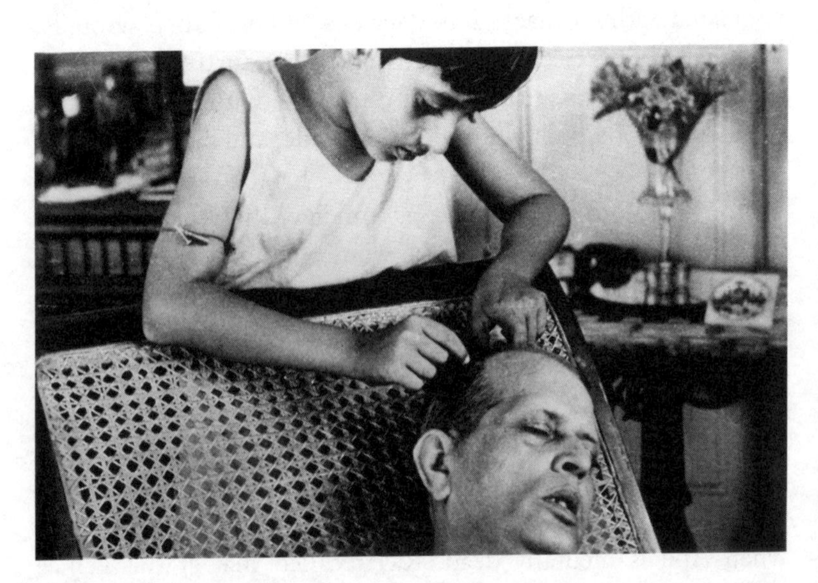

Aparajito: Sarbajaya, Apu and Harihar, just before he dies; Apu plucks grey hairs

for an orthodox Hindu like Harihar – the pigeons have a second, secular connotation: they open the film when Harihar emerges from the river, they surround him on the ghats, and so it seems natural and fitting that they should also close the final chapter of his life. The pigeons are not in the novel, as mentioned earlier. By choosing to focus on them, Ray, one feels, intended them to have this ambiguous meaning, which melds both Harihar's religious orthodoxy and Ray's own unorthodoxy in one uplifting poetic image.

After Harihar's cremation at the burning ghat in Benares – its rituals performed by his young son – Sarbajaya becomes a cook for a rich Bengali household, with Apu in tow, before she decides to leave the city for the village of her aged relative. This brief transitional period is handled with a cinematic finesse hard to do justice to in words. In one sequence, Apu is seen plucking the grey hairs of the head of the household while the man reclines dozing in the heat. Dismissively rewarded with a few coins to spend as he likes, Apu after a moment's thought dashes out of the mansion, steps nimbly through the ornate gate, passes through a local wedding procession accompanied by raucously exuberant music, buys some peanuts and enters a Hindu temple full of monkeys, which he happily feeds. As so often with Ray, nothing has really happened here – and virtually no words have been spoken – yet a character's shifting thoughts and moods have been exquisitely expressed. As the monkeys gambol and swing around the temple, snatch the food from Apu's eager hands and ring the temple bells with discordant abandon, Apu's curiosity and love of life are yet again impressed upon the mind of the viewer – in implied contradistinction to the resignation and fatalism of his mother Sarbajaya. In the final shot, the thought process in her decision to leave Benares is equally eloquent. Catching sight of Apu through the bars of a window behaving like a mere servant to the household, as she is coming down the stairs, she stops and then, pondering deeply, walks haltingly down the remaining steps, her face coming nearer and nearer to the camera until we can see her anguished expression in extreme close-up. Then, at the sound of a piercing train whistle, she half-turns, and the shot changes abruptly to a blurred view of passing railway carriages: we know Sarbajaya's mind is made up, and that she and Apu are now on their way to the new village.

As Ray remarked of his editing in an interview in 1958, before the Apu Trilogy was completed, 'I hate conventional time-lapses. They draw attention to themselves. I like strong modulations from one thing to another. You see, I am always hopefully concerned to get the feeling of the movement of life itself. There are no neat transitions in life. Things make the transition for me. A travelling train, for example. Again, there is no moment of evident transition, say, from childhood to boyhood, or on to youth.'

This comment pinpoints an underlying difficulty with *Aparajito* after the film leaves Benares. There are now several inevitable transitions in Apu's life as he grows up – becoming a young priest, going to school in the village, leaving for Calcutta to study science in college, taking his first real job in a printing press, and, of course, turning from a ten-year old (Pinaki Sen Gupta) into an adolescent (Smaran Ghosal). Some of them feel a little too neat. However, although Apu's general trajectory from rural obscurity to metropolitan enlightenment is predictable, like a Bengali David Copperfield, the specifics of the path he follows and the characters he meets on the way are not, which maintains our interest.

One irresistible scene, like the grocer–schoolmaster's school in *Pather Panchali*, shows the visit of a schools inspector. With Ray, formal education tends to be pictured as either monotonous or comic. Here comedy predominates, through many delicious touches, in particular the fastidious headmaster, a Christian in an immaculate black jacket and dhoti, shooing away a cow from the school courtyard by clapping his hands and shouting in English at the recalcitrant animal, shortly before the arrival by phaeton of the overdressed inspector, a beaming Bengali sahib in a white suit sporting a sola topee. The cow, however, gets her revenge, by reappearing at the very moment the honoured inspector reaches the school entrance. But then comedy gives way to seriousness. In front of the benign inspector and the anxious headmaster, Apu shines by reading with clarity and fervour a famous Bengali poem, '*Bangla Desh*' (Land of Bengal). Although this incident had its germ in Banerji's novel *Aparajito*, it was vividly developed by Ray, who chose the poem by Satyendranath Dutta. Perhaps he was thinking of a Ray family story. Satyajit's artist grandfather Upendrakisore, as a boy in East Bengal in the 1870s, had a school inspection by the governor of Bengal, who spotted the boy drawing intently in class. Picking up the book he saw an excellent sketch of himself. The boy's teachers were worried as to how the visiting British sahib would react. But the governor patted Upendrakisore on the back and told him, in English: 'You must not let this skill disappear. When you grow up you should follow this line.'

Education divides Apu from his mother in the latter half of *Aparajito*, as we know. The most poignant sequence in their relationship occurs when he returns to the village for the first time since starting college in Calcutta. Sarbajaya is sitting listlessly sewing beneath a tree. As the train from Calcutta comes beetling across the near horizon, she busies herself to receive Apu. A solo *sarangi*, the most piercing of the Indian string instruments, expresses her loneliness with heart-wrenching pathos. She is still drawing water from the well when Apu arrives. Instead of pulling the bucket up, she simply lets the rope snap back in her joy; no embrace could have been more eloquent, especially given the calm way in which we have seen her draw water in *Pather Panchali*.

Apu is genuinely pleased to see his mother, but the gap between them is evident from the moment he arrives. He has barely exchanged a few sentences with her before he is off for a dip in the village pond. That night as she sits fanning Apu at his evening meal, as once she fanned her husband Harihar, Sarbajaya

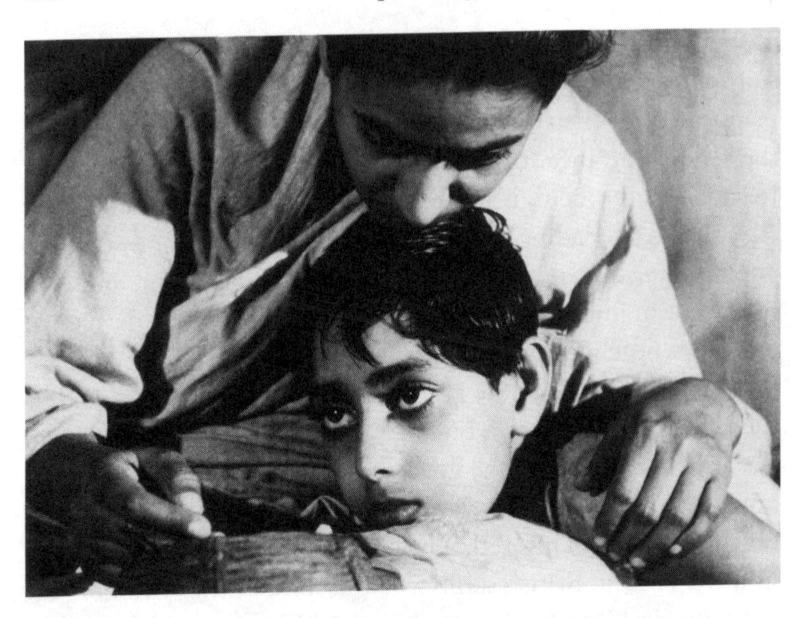

Aparajito: Apu and education. Apu with his mother Sarbajaya; and with his headmaster

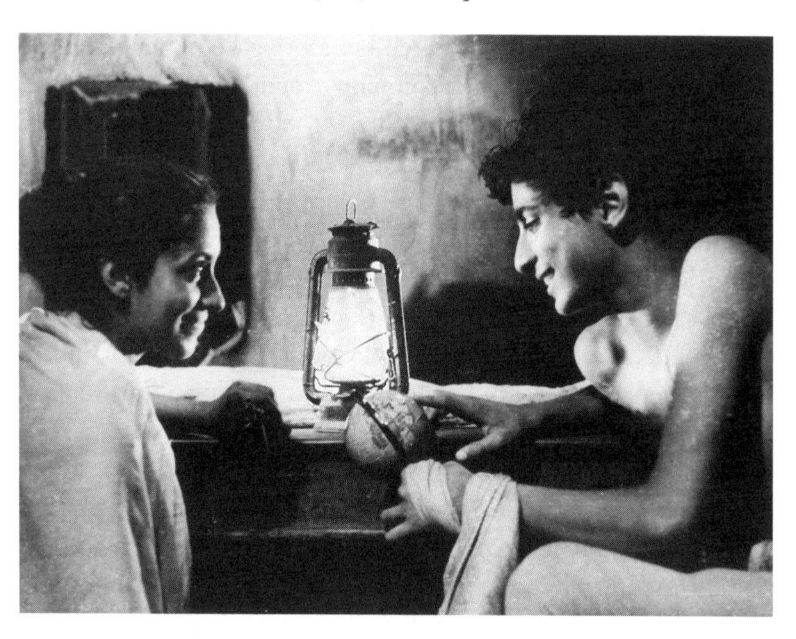

longs for him to open up and tell her all that he has experienced in Calcutta. They grope for common ground. Apu reassures her that he still prefers her cooking. Later, he reads, she sews. With some asperity she tells him to put his book away and talk to her about what he has seen. He recites a list of Calcutta place names almost meaningless to her and adds, with a yawn: 'Keoratala'. 'What's there at Keoratala?' enquires Sarbajaya. 'Burning ghat,' says Apu, in English. This makes his mother pensive. She wonders out loud what has obviously been on her mind in Apu's absence: what will happen to her if she falls ill? Will Apu look after her? she asks. Of course, he will, Apu says, without thinking. Sarbajaya presses him: 'You're not going to come to me and leave your studies, are you? Will you arrange for my treatment with the money you earn? Will you, Apu?' But Apu has gone to sleep. Immediately, we remember another such scene, in *Pather Panchali*, when Harihar drifted off to sleep while Sarbajaya delivered herself of her worries. We know instinctively that Sarbajaya has not got long to live and the music reinforces this – it is the first time since Harihar's death in Benares that we hear the flute playing the melody in raga *Jog*, here in a gentler variation.

'Goodness knows how many films have used the snuffed out candle to suggest death', Ray once wrote, ' – but the really effective language is both fresh and vivid at the same time, and the search for it an inexhaustible one.' In Banerji's novel, on her deathbed Sarbajaya has a vision of Apu as a child. Ray adopted this hint and transformed it for the cinema. In the twilight of evening, the dying Sarbajaya hears the whistle of a train passing, and then the voice of the adolescent Apu calling her. She rises heavily to her feet, looks out of the door in hope – but there is no one there, only the glimmering pond, the empty path along which Apu has so often walked from the station, and sparkling fireflies. Sarbajaya sinks down on the threshold in despair. The screen goes black, except for the fireflies. As the points of light dart around, darkness covers the trees, the pond and the path, like a shroud.

Aparajito: Sarbajaya and neighbour, not long before Sarbajaya's death

The final scene – Apu's return, too late, to Mansapota – does not directly portray his mingling of grief and joy, so crucial to the novel. Ray is too oblique an artist for this. Apu's state of mind emerges not from his words, but from his actions. Instead of staying in the village to perform his mother's memorial rituals, as expected by his ageing uncle, he packs up his mother's few possessions and departs again for Calcutta to take his college examinations. Apu will perform the rituals in the city, he informs his uncle, not remain in the village as a priest. The last we see of him he is walking, alone, back along the familiar path, now bare-foot out of traditional respect for his late mother, gradually disappearing into the distance to the accompaniment of a flute hesitantly playing the main theme of *Pather Panchali*. Though churning inside, not for one instant does Apu look back.

7

The World of Apu: Critique

When India's prime minister Jawaharlal Nehru saw *Aparajito* at a private screening, just before its general release in Calcutta in 1956, he came over and congratulated Ray, and unexpectedly asked him: 'What happens to Apu now?' Ray answered that he did not have a third film in mind. Then, at the Venice Film Festival in 1957, during a press conference before the screening of *Aparajito* (and before it won the top prize), Ray found himself, when asked the same question by a journalist, giving a different answer – without really meaning it – to the effect that he did have a trilogy in mind. Nevertheless, it took him a fair while to get around to making the third film. After the completion of two other films in 1957–58 (*The Philosopher's Stone* and *The Music Room*), *The World of Apu* was eventually shot in 1958–59.

No trace of this hesitation appears on the screen. Whereas *Pather Panchali* has some obvious technical flaws (of which Ray was only too acutely aware, as we know), and *Aparajito* has significant weaknesses in its Calcutta scenes, *The World of Apu* is a wonderfully fluent film, well-nigh faultless in every department of its production, from the performances of the principals – Soumitra Chatterji as Apu and Sharmila Tagore as Aparna – and

The World of Apu: Apu in his garret

the smallest parts, to the script, camerawork, lighting, art direction, editing and music by Ravi Shankar. The result is a work one virtually cannot avoid being moved by: 'surely one of the most moving films ever made', wrote Robin Wood in his study *The Apu Trilogy*.

Consider the opening scene, following the credits. (There is a brief prologue before the credits.) Without a word being spoken, Apu's character and situation are established through effortless use of details in and around his rooftop garret, which seem so natural that they never draw unnecessary attention to themselves. The lighting shows that it is morning. The very first image is of a wet window curtain with a big tear in the cloth, flapping in the wind as rain pours down outside. Plainly Apu is poor; and he also cannot be bothered with domestic matters. A piercing train whistle and shunting sounds, close by, awaken him from sleep on his basic-looking bedstead. His accommodation clearly abuts a railway yard. A sheaf of papers, an upturned ink bottle, a dark blotch on his disordered bedsheet and his vest, and a bare electric bulb on the wall that is still burning subtly suggest that he is now a would-be writer who must have fallen asleep over his manuscript while writing at night. Getting up quickly, he investigates the damage, hastily takes the soiled sheet outdoors onto the terrace to soak it in a bucket, is briefly distracted by the whistles and movement of a nearby train below, then looks over the parapet and sees a woman down below in the courtyard on the ground floor fiddling with a water tap; immediately, he decides not to bother going all the way downstairs and back for water, and with a touch of imagination shoves the bucket under a stream of rainwater gushing from a roof gutter onto the terrace. His cleaning problem temporarily solved, he now gives himself a free shower by happily standing in the downpour while doing physical jerks. Apu's abandon in the rain, plus the bareness and untidiness of his room, together suggest a youthful capacity to take pleasure in simple things whilst letting his mind roam over higher matters – like the boy Apu we have seen in *Pather Panchali* and *Aparajito*.

But the brute facts of existence soon reassert themselves. There is an introductory cough at the door, as Apu stands in the midst of shaving. His landlord, a late middle-aged man with a receding hairline, a calculating face and pursed lips who leans on a stick – the physical antithesis of Apu – enters. He speaks to his tenant civilly enough but with a faint whiff of menace:

Landlord: Namaskar!
Apu: (*casually, continuing to shave*) Namaskar. Take a seat.
Landlord: Will taking a seat do any good, Apurba Babu?
Apu: It'll rest your tired limbs. Walking up three flights of stairs is hard work.
Landlord: (*with a mirthless smile*) I haven't come up all those stairs to rest my limbs. You know as well as I do what I've come for. I'll put a straight question to

you; you give me a straight answer, and all our troubles will be over.

Apu: Go ahead.

Landlord: (*sternly*) What is the date today?

Apu: The tenth.

Landlord: And how many months' rent do you owe me?

Apu: Three.

Landlord: Three. Three times seven, makes twenty-one rupees. Do I get the money now, or do I have to come back in the evening?

Apu: That makes three questions, not one. It's not fair.

Landlord: A lot of things are not fair, Apurba Babu. Is it fair that I should house you for nothing? Is it fair that you should burn up precious electricity in the day-time? You have had education. You have pictures of great men hanging on the wall. Is it fair that you don't pay the rent?

Apu: It's a sign of greatness, you know.

Landlord: (*coughing*) I can't win a battle of words with you, Apurba Babu. I could turn a pretty phrase too, but it won't be fit for your young ears. Anyway, I'll come back this evening. Either I get my money, or I shall look for a new lodger.

Apu: Straight talk.

Landlord: Straight talk.

As he exits the room, the landlord pointedly switches off the light. Apu promptly switches it on again, and then, childishly, goes outside and switches on a second, equally otiose light.

This is the landlord's only appearance in *The World of Apu*, yet his is a remarkably substantial presence. Not only because of the nuanced performance, but also because Ray shows at least some sympathy for the character. 'The awful thing about life is this: Everyone has his reasons.' – Jean Renoir said famously (through his role as Octave) in *The Rules of the Game*. Ray fully agreed with Renoir. Deliberately, he divides our sympathy between Apu and the landlord and keeps it in exquisite tension in the little scene, as he continues to do in every scene of the film. Writers are important to society, Ray seems to say, whether practical people like landlords acknowledge this truth or not – but writers too have obligations to others, not only to their talent. While there is no doubt, in the film as a whole, that Ray is on the side of Apu, the creative artist – not of the landlord, sweatshop employers and their dull employees, his manipulative friend Pulu and Pulu's conventional relatives whom Apu encounters, even at times his beloved wife Aparna – Ray is careful never to tilt the balance entirely in Apu's favour against the philistines. As a rule, villains bored him, Ray once said – and there is not a single villain in his oeuvre, except in his two detective films (*The Golden Fortress/Sonar Kella* and *The Elephant God/Joi Baba Felunath*) and his two musicals (*The Adventures of Goopy and Bagha/Goopy Gyne Bagha Byne* and *The Kingdom of Diamonds/Hirak Rajar Dese*), which were all made with children in mind.

The theme of the first scene is explicitly developed a little further on, during the late evening. Apu's college friend Pulu has determinedly tracked Apu down to his lonely garret. Thanks to Pulu, who has rather more money than Apu, they have had a filling meal – Apu's first in ages – and have just paid a visit to the theatre, where they saw a well-loved nineteenth-century Bengali farce about an intellectual drunkard (*Sadhabar Ekadasi* by Dinabandhu Mitra). Apu is feeling light-headed, high not on alcohol but on his literary aspirations. Spotted by a suspicious patrolling policeman, feigning bravado Apu spouts an absurd soliloquy from the play in the constable's general direction – imitating the main character in the farce, who spouts Shakespeare and Milton at a British policeman – and then skedaddles with Pulu. In a long tracking shot, the friends amble along the tracks of the railway yard late at night, discussing life, literature and love.

At Pulu's request, Apu expatiates on the novel he is writing in his room. Like many first novels, it turns out to be autobiographical. A village boy, 'poor, but *sensitive*' (the second adjective is spoken in English by Apu), whose late father was a priest, decides to study hard, come to the city, shed his old superstitions, learn to use his intellect and imagination, and strive for greatness. Although he does not achieve this, and remains poor, he does not run away from responsibility but instead 'learns to *live*!', says Apu excitedly. The stolid Pulu is unconvinced: where is the novelist's invention, he asks. A lot of it is fiction, responds Apu, with imaginary characters, a plot and love interest. What can Apu possibly know about love, says a crushing Pulu. 'Have you ever been within ten yards of a girl?' (A line that would obviously have been impossible, had Ray included Apu's girlfriend Lila in *Aparajito*, as originally intended.) Surely imagination counts in writing novels, as well as experience, insists Apu hotly. Not where love is concerned, replies Pulu bluntly. They quarrel in a friendly way in the silent railway yard – and we realise how naively romantic about the world Apu is.

In the very next scene, Apu is on his way by boat with Pulu to the family wedding in the riverine village away from Calcutta, with fateful consequences. We first see Aparna as a young, bashful bride being decorated for her wedding by her mother and the other women of the family. Apu is outside all of this ceremony, but the way in which he is included in the camera movement and editing of the sequence implies that he will eventually be drawn into the wedding. The wedding band arrives, escorting the bridegroom's marriage party along the bank beside the river. Above them, at the top of the bank, as the camera follows the party below, we eventually come to Apu stretched out beneath a tree in a doze, with his head on a collection of Tagore's poetry and his flute in his hand, like the god Krishna on the banks of the Kalindi. The band plays their own raucous version of 'For He's A Jolly Good Fellow' – strange, perhaps, to western ears in this rustic Indian context, but quite familiar to Bengali ears used

The World of Apu: Aparna's mother and Aparna as a bride; Apu and Aparna on their wedding night

to hearing it at the annual immersion of the Durga image during the Durga Puja festival in Calcutta (although the English words are long since lost). This juxtaposition of Apu and the band is enriched by our earlier memory of Apu listening to a wedding band play 'Tipperary' in *Pather Panchali*; but in those far-off days he was thrilled by the sight, whereas now he is blasé, Calcutta-returned.

The bridegroom turns out to be mad, of course, and Apu has to come to the rescue of Aparna by marrying her himself. The psychology of his decision was discussed earlier (in chapter 2), but not its aftermath, which begins with one of the most touching scenes in the film.

Immediately after the wedding, Apu and Aparna are seen alone for the first time, standing apart from each other in a flower-strewn bedroom. A western viewer naturally assumes that their inaugural togetherness follows on the various marriage prayers and vows, but in fact a traditional Hindu couple must await the third night of their wedding; in between, they sleep separately, the bride surrounded by her female relations, the groom by his male ones. When the third night comes, custom lays down that the groom be alone with the bride in his own house. Apu is too poor to do this. As he tells Aparna: 'Have you ever heard of a bride and groom spending their *phulsajya* ['bed of flowers'] in the bride's home?' Not surprisingly, he feels that he is there on false pretences – does Aparna know anything about the man she has married? His mood is self-lacerating, as plangent boatmen's songs come drifting through the window from the dark river outside; but at the point where Aparna softly tells him that she can accept poverty, he lightens up with a joke about his Calcutta neighbours: 'I told them I was going to a wedding, and now I'm returning with the bride!' Her transparent devotion having won him over, the poignant *esraj* expressing their love (in raga *Lachari Todi*) changes into the fast rhythm of the sitar initially used to express bachelor Apu's carefree nature as he walked back to his room along the railway tracks near the beginning of the film.

The World of Apu: Apu and Aparna's return to Calcutta, ignored by his downstairs neighbour

The series of short scenes in Calcutta lasting about 20 minutes that show the new couple together are, in Robin Wood's phrase, 'one of the cinema's classic affirmative depictions of married life.' Through her love, Aparna finally convinces a disbelieving Apu that she does not regret marrying a man without money or possessions. Part of the pathos derives from the fact that the scenes take place in the very same physical surroundings in which we came to know Apu the bachelor. Almost unconsciously, we compare. As Apu emerges from inside playing his flute (a Tagore melody well known in Bengal later used in a hit Hindi film), and observes every little action of Aparna as she prepares to cook on her brazier, we inevitably think of Apu as a bachelor lying alone on a rumpled bed, shyly closing the shutter of the window against the stare of the girl next door with the tip of his flute on which he plays a quite different melody, just before Pulu bursts in on his life.

Each of these scenes dissolves magically into the next. As Renoir remarked, when he saw the film in Paris, intimacy is suggested without showing a single embrace. Finally, after husband and wife have been out to see a hammy mythological film – in which the antics of the gods embarrass the sophisticated Apu but enthral his more traditional wife – the cinema screen segues into the back window of a horse-drawn carriage, and they are alone again in their lovers' world. The intimate understanding and precise shifts of mood in their conversation inside the cab can only partially be conveyed by subtitles, but the scene nevertheless remains one of the high points of the film, accompanied by the same musical transition as after the wedding – from the *esraj* playing Apu and Aparna's theme to the sitar in carefree mood. When Aparna strikes a match to light the cigarette that Apu has unthinkingly put in his mouth (forgetting his promise to his wife to smoke only after meals), he notices that the flame has brought a strange and wonderful glow to her face. 'What is there in your eyes?' he asks with tenderness. 'Kohl,' she answers mischievously, according to the English subtitle. But in Bengali she says '*Kajal*', which is the word for kohl or mascara. It is also the name of the baby son she will soon bear Apu and who will cause her death. A vital link of emotion and artistry in the film is thereby lost on the western viewer, for whom the pun is unavoidably untranslatable. The double-meaning could be read as the subtlest of suggestions that Apu, after long rejecting Kajal, will in the end embrace him. Satyajit Ray is among the most natural and nuanced writers of dialogue the cinema has produced, but unfortunately only Bengali-speakers can fully savour this pleasure.

Apu's suicide attempt on the railway tracks – which forms no part of the novel *Aparajito* – after he receives the stunning news of Aparna's death, is powerfully and originally dramatised in the film. We see the build-up, with Apu lying immobile on his bed, indifferent to food, books or people. His downstairs neighbour, a matronly woman, loses no time in advising him that he should

The World of Apu: Apu and Aparna as husband and wife

marry again. He certainly has his reasons to take his own life, and yet his moment of decision seems to depend not on reason, nor even on emotion, but on a chance event: the stopping of his bedside clock. (Chance will also save him, in the shape of a wandering pig that is killed by the train on the tracks just ahead of him with a blood-curdling squeal.) The clock stops ticking while Apu is staring at his haggard reflection in the mirror; some silent seconds pass, then he hears the long mournful whistle of a train and turns slightly towards the sound; he now knows the method by which he will kill himself. This shot recalls the very similar moment in *Aparajito* when Sarbajaya happens to see Apu behaving like a servant, ponders silently, hears a train whistle, turns slightly towards the sound, and decides to leave Benares. Both shots plumb the unfathomable nature of thinking to a depth found in the work of very few other directors.

Somewhat less convincing, at least in my view (and that of Robin Wood), is the style of Apu's renunciation of all his ties to Calcutta, including his unfinished novel, after he decides to live. Travelling away from the city by train, he journeys to the coast, the forest and the hills to find freedom from his old life. As Ray explained:

> The fact of the death of the wife in childbirth is obviously a traumatic experience for him. An experience like that can bring about very strong, far-reaching changes in a man's outlook on life and death and the meaning of existence etc. He's absolutely shattered by the death because it happens so quickly. And the next step – that's very Indian. Probably it doesn't appeal to the West so much, but I think it's probably in keeping with Indian philosophy and the Indian attitude to life. Certainly in Bibhutibhusan [Banerji] it's very strong. Anyway, I'm quite happy with the transition from a mood of suicide to a mood of renunciation.

Apu's renunciation, his immersion in nature and his odyssey around India are indeed integral to the novel at this point. 'Being

The World of Apu: Apu's renunciation; Pulu and Apu

alone in these isolated places brought a change in his own state of mind', Banerji writes of Apu. 'In the city, one's mind might be wholly preoccupied with thoughts of self, desire or ambition. Here, under the colossal expanse of the star-studded sky, these things seemed both irrelevant and insignificant. ... Even books that had once seemed fascinating, or important in his busy life in the city, now appeared trivial, dull, unnecessary in his present seclusion.' The real difficulty comes with Ray's treatment of Apu's novel, which does not exist in Banerji's book prior to Aparna's death; he begins writing it during his period of renunciation, as mentioned before. In the film, Apu, arriving at sunrise on the top of a hill, takes the sheets of his manuscript from his cloth bag and lets them float away down the hillside on the wind like confetti. Even for such an intensely romantic Bengali as Apu, this symbolic gesture seems implausible – more pretentious than profound. (To future generations, unaware because of computers of how only a single copy of an author's work could exist, the gesture may appear literally unintelligible.) Whatever justification may be offered for it, the incident undoubtedly can derive no direct support from Banerji's novel.

This false note apart, the remainder of the film is pitch perfect. Back in the village, we see Kajal for the first time since he was a tiny baby. Or rather, we do not see him, because his face is hidden by a frightening, shark-like mask. With a catapult, the masked figure kills a bird, walks up to it in bare feet, pulls the mask back, picks the dead creature up by one leg, inspects its corpse, and makes a toothy grimace at it, reminiscent of the teeth painted on his mask. The combination of life and lifelessness, innocence and cruelty, delicacy and clumsiness, in this close-up of the angelic-looking child and the dead bird – accompanied by playful, yet somehow alien music – is an introduction to Kajal even more compelling than our first meetings with the boy Apu in *Pather Panchali* and *Aparajito*. There is a wildness in Apu's son, not found in Apu himself, due to his orphaned upbringing at the hands of his resentful, disciplinarian grandfather; but his

The World of Apu: Kajal

behaviour with the bird and in a subsequent scene with an angry neighbour seems to be a mask concealing a sensitivity like his father's, and not his true nature.

Pulu, recently returned from abroad and currently on a visit to his uncle's house, is seen watching the difficult little boy. Despite the uncle's pessimism about both his son-in-law Apu and grandson Kajal, Pulu is moved to try to break through Apu's own mask of indifference to his son. He seeks out Apu in the stark, hilly landscape near a coal mine far from Calcutta where Apu is working, as once he sought him out in his garret in Calcutta. But this time Pulu fails in his mission. He cannot comprehend why Apu has destroyed the novel Pulu had once read and greatly admired. And he is shocked that Apu does not care to know even the name of his son. When Pulu tells him of Kajal, Apu cannot bring himself to show any pity for the boy. 'It is because Kajal exists, that Aparna does not,' he finally tells his friend, choking back violent emotions.

The World of Apu: finale. Apu, Kajal and Kajal's grandfather

Yet, against Apu's will, seeing and hearing Pulu after an age has churned him. The village section at the end of the film in which Apu at last returns to the place of his wedding to see Kajal for the first time is marvellous in its deployment of the total resources of cinema. It comprises the most emotionally saturated scenes in Ray's entire oeuvre, bearing the full history of Apu's life and struggle up to this point. As he sits upstairs in his father-in-law's house watching the little boy who does not know him asleep on the bed, the boatmen's songs again drift in off the river; we cannot help but think of another occasion in this same room. Then, Aparna's devotion penetrated Apu's protective shell. Can her child now do the same, and displace the icon of his dead mother that Apu has preserved in his heart?

The boy's rejection of this unkempt stranger is at first total; Apu's every attempt at friendliness is rebuffed. When he claims that he is Kajal's father, the boy actually throws a stone at him. Only when, without thinking, Apu goes to Kajal's rescue as his irascible grandfather is about to punish the boy by beating him with his heavy stick, is a spark of trust ignited for a moment. But it does not catch fire. And then, as Apu sets off alone along the riverbank leaving Kajal behind, it becomes a flame. Like his friend Pulu, who in more or less the same spot requested him to marry Aparna and was at first refused outright, Apu has given up on Kajal. But Kajal, with a child's instinct, has decided to trust this bearded man and follows behind him as he departs. 'Will you take me to my father?' he calls out. 'Will my father be cross with me?' 'He won't leave me and go away?' Then, finally, the hardest question: 'Who are you?' Apu replies, with a tremor of hesitation: 'I'm your – friend. Will you come with me?' Watched by his grandfather in the distance, the boy runs to Apu and is swept up in his arms to the piercing notes of a high *tar-shehnai*, heard only once before in the Trilogy, when Apu's parents, Harihar and Sarbajaya, wept over the death of Durga. It is as if the love that was snuffed out then has, after long years, been rekindled. Through Kajal, Apu has transcended his grief at last and is a better, more whole person. The music that plays out *The World of Apu*, as Apu carries off his son on his shoulders to a new life together, expresses this complex of emotions: the basic notes are recognisable as those of the Apu–Aparna theme last heard in the carriage in their final hours together, but now they have acquired a nobility and serenity of emotion more reminiscent of a hymn.

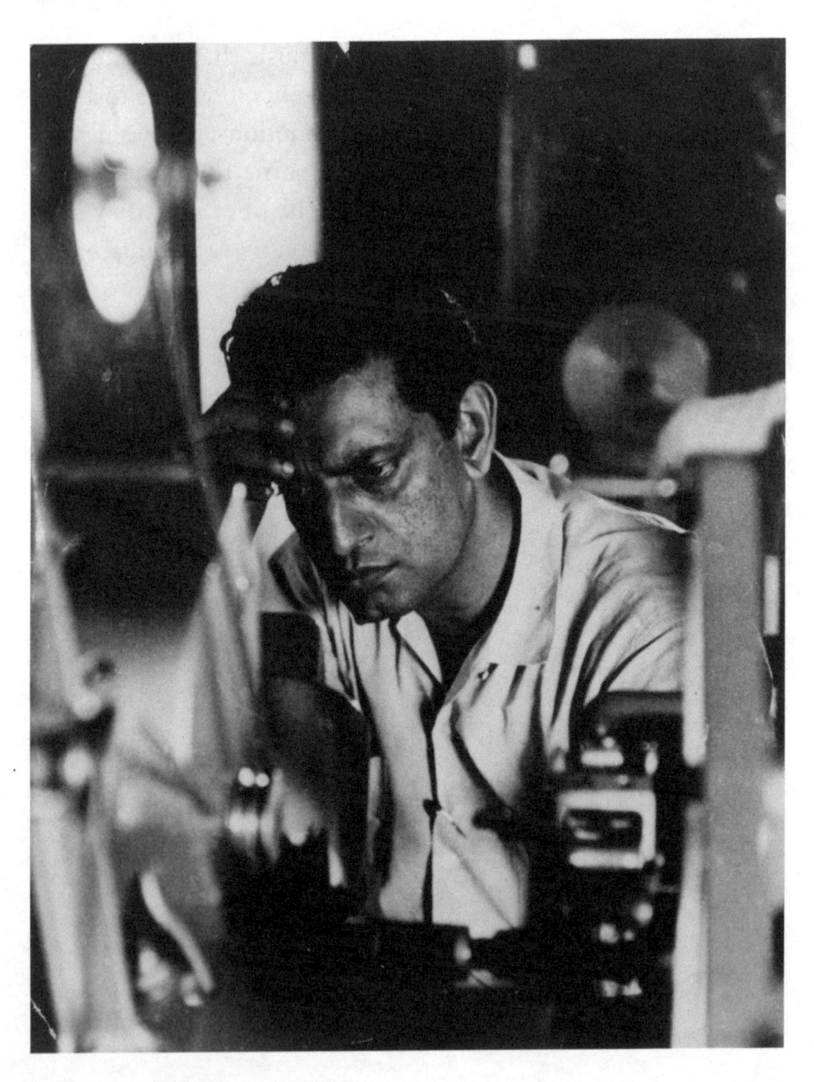

Ray at the editing table, in mid-career

8

From Calcutta to Cannes: The Reception of the Apu Trilogy

In the decades after the release of the Apu Trilogy in the 1950s, beginning with *Pather Panchali* in Bengal in 1955, two myths grew up about its original reception. One was that it was a failure in India until its success in the West. The other was that its success in the West was immediate and unqualified. Both myths were fostered by two unquestionable facts. First, Satyajit Ray's films always had a very small market in India compared to Bollywood films – which helped to make the first myth plausible. Secondly, the artistic distinction of his films was always far more widely appreciated by western critics and audiences than by Indian ones – which obviously encouraged the second myth. However, neither myth is actually supported by the historical evidence. Although the Indian and western reception of *Pather Panchali*, and the Apu Trilogy as a whole, was fairly complicated, as a generalisation it is true that *Pather Panchali* was a triumphant success in Bengal in 1955 and that the Apu Trilogy divided western critics and audiences into fervent admirers and apathetic detractors, beginning with the film festival juries at Cannes in 1956 and at Venice in 1957. As a further generalisation, the official class in India showed a shameful, philistine indifference or opposition to *Pather Panchali*, redeemed only by the personal admiration of Prime Minister Nehru, his daughter Indira Gandhi and a few enlightened civil servants and diplomats able to see beyond its depiction of poverty.

The world premiere of *Pather Panchali* took place, as we know, at the Museum of Modern Art in New York, in May 1955. Very few Indians were in the audience, but there was one, a Bengali acquaintance of Ray from Calcutta Film Society days, Bidyut Sarkar, who wrote to him from the United States immediately after the screening. 'My emotions after seeing *Pather Panchali* were mixed', recalled Sarkar in 1992, in his small book on Ray's films. 'I felt elated myself, but it did not seem to have stirred the audience as a whole, which disappointed me. The fresh print we saw was yet to be subtitled; nor was a synopsis presented to the viewers.' A worried Ray – who was yet to hear back from his sponsors at the MoMA – promptly replied, agreeing with Sarkar that *Pather Panchali* needed a short but well-informed introduction, 'preferably by myself', to prepare a western audience. 'Without this, the film was bound to fall flat – especially on an American audience.' However, he continued, 'when all is said and done, I cannot believe that the really sensitive among the audience could have entirely failed to respond to the many touches and details which I have attempted in the film. I was glad to note that you have mentioned some of these in your letter.'

This reaction was certainly true of Monroe Wheeler, the curator at MoMA who had originally invited Ray to send his film, and also of Wheeler's colleague Richard Griffith, the curator in charge of the museum's film library, who was so impressed he volunteered to screen the film for potential US distributors. Only one distributor, Edward Harrison, who was already a promoter of Japanese cinema (Akira Kurosawa and Kenji Mizoguchi) in America, fell for *Pather Panchali*; he subsequently became a complete devotee of Ray, visiting his shooting in India in 1961 and releasing all his films in the United States until his premature death in 1967. ('I think Ed was one of those rare human beings who must be classed under the category of Essentially Good Men in spite of being rabid reactionaries,' Ray wrote at the time in a letter to his first biographer Marie Seton.) But despite Harrison's enthusiasm, he was unable to persuade any New York theatre to give *Pather Panchali* a first run until the latter half of 1958 – and then only, it appears, by agreeing to put up a guarantee.

We already know (from chapter 3) of the success of *Pather Panchali* in Calcutta in the autumn of 1955, following its premiere in New York. Not only did it fill the cinema houses for many weeks and become the talk of the town, it also impressed the Bengali commercial film industry. On the strength of its box-office receipts, Ray received a proposal from a Bengali producer, boss of one of the large Calcutta studios, that he should direct five films for him. He was tempted to accept but was unable to come to an agreement on rates for his production team that he felt were acceptable, and so the deal fell through.

Despite sustained opposition from within both the West Bengal Government – the producer of *Pather Panchali* – and the Government of India in New Delhi, because of the film's stark portrayal of poverty, *Pather Panchali* was sent to the Cannes Film Festival in May 1956 after important efforts on its behalf by Marie Seton (who had seen the film in Delhi and travelled to Calcutta in late 1955 to meet Ray in person). Although the choice of *Pather Panchali* to represent India abroad had the personal approval of Nehru, nothing was done by the government to promote the film at the festival; there was not even the usual launch party.

By a quirk of fate, *Pather Panchali*'s unheralded screening at Cannes clashed with a party given by the Japanese delegation for a film by Kurosawa, and so there was a poor turnout. But some critics who did see it – including Lindsay Anderson (from Britain), André Bazin and Lotte Eisner (from France), and Gene Moskowitz (from the United States) – were thrilled by the film and incensed that its Indian origin and lack of official support meant that it would be overlooked for a prize.

In his review of the Cannes Festival for the London *Observer*, Anderson enthused most of all about *Pather Panchali*:

> The festival finished with a week of big names, yet the outstanding achievement came from an unknown. This is the best kind of surprise. Cannes 1956 has discovered a new masterpiece of poetic cinema.... With apparent formlessness, *Pather Panchali* traces the great designs of life.... You cannot make films like this in a studio, nor for money. Satyajit Ray has worked with humility and complete dedication; he has gone down on his knees in the dust. And his picture has the quality of intimate, unforgettable experience.

Eisner wrote in her diary for May 7:

> Here is the discovery of the festival: *Lament of the Road* (*Pather Panchali*) from India. A Bengali film by Satyajit Ray, who, incidentally, worked with Jean Renoir on *The River*. Here is great purity and a surprising cinematic lyricism. It is one of those rare works in which nothing seems to happen, but where we feel we are being given a piece of life itself, unembellished, where we see before our eyes people living their daily lives with their small joys and their great affliction. All this without false exoticism, with honesty, and without exaggerating the facts.... Satyajit Ray [is] the Flaherty of Bengal...

Three days later, Eisner noted that the major awards had gone mostly to French films, but that *Pather Panchali* had won a minor prize. In her opinion, Ray's film should have taken the top prize, the Golden Palm.

Pather Panchali's prize had come about as a result of pressure from influential critics, who forced a rescreening of Ray's film. Then the British member of the festival jury, James Quinn (a notably cultured director of the British Film Institute), along with two other jury members, put forward *Pather Panchali* as worthy of a prize. 'The initial reaction was one of shock if not of horror by most of those present,' Quinn recalled in the 1980s, 'especially the French scriptwriter Henri Jaenson [*Un Carnet de Bal*] who referred to *Pather Panchali* as "*cette ordure*" – as I vividly remember.' But *Pather Panchali* was too good for French hubris to kill it off; it was awarded a special prize, for 'Best Human Document'. (Nevertheless, Ray's films were pointedly ignored in France, especially by the New Wave directors like François Truffaut and Jean-Luc Godard, until the early 1980s, when there was a sudden upsurge of French interest in Ray.)

Understandably, Ray himself did not feel he had truly arrived in the international cinema until *Aparajito* won the Golden Lion at Venice, the following year. The award was all the more welcome for being wholly unexpected; in Bengal, as we know, *Aparajito* had not enjoyed anything like the success of its predecessor, probably because its portrait of the mother–son relationship (Sarbajaya and Apu) was so unsparing and lacking in conventional pieties. By and large, *Aparajito* upset the Bengali middle class: the people Ray had grown up with. He himself felt the film had some technical failings – in the soundtrack especially, as a result of Ravi Shankar's rushed composition of the music. He recalled 'squirming' in his seat in the 6,000-seater Grande Salle during the Venice Festival screening. 'It was a formal occasion and in the balcony sat Henry Fonda, Maria Callas, Toshiro Mifune and a host of celebrities.' But the audience reaction, usherettes included, was good. Still, Ray had 'not the slightest hope of winning any prizes'. Three days before the award ceremony a journalist gave Ray a whispered hint – 'I can hear the lion's roar' – then on the afternoon of the day itself, 'a young girl of pronounced good looks came to our hotel, sought us out and started briefing me on what I had to do on the stage that evening. "On the stage?" I asked. "Yes," she said, "your name will be called out and you come up to take the prize." "What prize?" "Leone d'Oro."' According to Ray, he kept his cool with some effort, but his Bengali companion, Santi Choudhury, who had paid for *Aparajito*'s subtitling in Italian, sprang up and kissed the Italian girl smack on the lips.

Again, it had been a British member of the jury, Penelope Houston, editor of *Sight and Sound*, who wanted Ray's film to win. After much argument, the chairman, French director René Clair, acquiesced with good grace; but on the boat back from the jury's meeting place to the awards ceremony, Houston remembered Clair saying to her – without a trace of malice towards *Aparajito*'s director: 'But now I hope Ray will go away and learn how to make films'!

Because of delays in subtitling, *Pather Panchali* did not open in London until Christmas 1957, at the Academy Cinema, now trailing its laurels from Cannes and Venice (for *Aparajito*, which followed at the same theatre in February 1958). It ran well and its reviews were almost uniformly outstanding, despite an element of discomfort with the poverty of the family and especially with the film's slow pace, epitomised by one review carrying the headline 'So much beauty yet I had to yawn'. Dilys Powell, writing in the *Sunday Times*, was probably typical in her reaction. She had seen *Pather Panchali* at Cannes (presumably at its second screening) somewhat reluctantly but admitted immediately afterwards: 'Now that I look back on the festival it is of *Pather Panchali* that I think: the forest, the lake, the children growing up, the train whose whistle speaks to them of escape.' Reviewing it again 18 months later, Powell discovered that the film had grown on her:

> at a second look... one realises better how subtly one's attention is directed ahead. An old life shrivels and dies; the watching boy and girl by every action, every moment of observation, are preparing for their own lives.... [*Pather Panchali*] has the time-sense of childhood, that period when tiny happenings

are as urgent as great ones, when some trivial incident, a letter, a train passing, the wind singing in a telegraph pole, can seem to last eternally.

But it was in the United States, the following autumn, that *Pather Panchali* had its biggest success – on a scale that no other film by Ray would ever again enjoy outside of Bengal. It had already won an award for Best Film and Direction at the 1957 San Francisco Film Festival. Now, in September 1958, distributed by the loyal Harrison, the film opened at the Fifth Avenue Cinema in New York. Ray, who had been invited to the United States by Robert Flaherty's widow for the Flaherty film seminar in Vermont, was present in the theatre lobby for the opening night. In 1982, he recalled the occasion in *Sight and Sound*:

> I watched the audience surge out of the theatre blear-eyed and visibly shaken. An hour or so later, in the small hours, came the morning edition of the *New York Times*. It carried Bosley Crowther's review of my film. Crowther was the doyen of New York critics, with power to make or mar a film's prospects as a saleable commodity. Crowther was unmoved by *Pather Panchali*. In fact, he said the film was so amateurish that 'it would barely pass for a rough cut in Hollywood.' Later, he had second thoughts as letters poured in to say how wrong he was. The film ran for eight months. And yet I know Crowther was not wholly wrong. Judged on the level of craftsmanship, there was much that was wrong with my film.

It is worth looking closely at Crowther's review, which was by no means all negative, because it is a quintessential example of a clash between film cultures that remains more than pertinent half a century later. Ray had decided back in 1950, when he started *Pather Panchali* after seeing *Bicycle Thieves* and *The Rules of the Game* in London, that: 'The entire conventional approach (as exemplified by even the best American and British films) is wrong' – as explained in chapter 1. *Pather Panchali*'s technical inadequacies aside, to an American critic like Crowther schooled in Hollywood films of the period, Ray's European inspiration, combined with his wholly unfamiliar Bengali setting, rendered *Pather Panchali* almost incomprehensible.

Here is Crowther's 500-word *New York Times* review, published on 23 September, in its entirety:

> The Indian film, *Pather Panchali* (*Song of the Road*), which opened at the Fifth Avenue Cinema yesterday, is one of those rare exotic items, remote in idiom from the usual Hollywood film, that should offer some subtle compensations to anyone who has the patience to sit through its almost two hours.
>
> Chief among the delicate revelations that emerge from its loosely formed account of the pathetic little joys and sorrows of a poor Indian family in Bengal is the touching indication that poverty does not always nullify love and that even the most afflicted people can find some modest pleasures in their worlds. This theme, which is not as insistent or sentimental as it may sound, barely begins to be evident after the picture has run at least an hour. And, in that time, the most the camera shows us in a rambling and random tour of an Indian village is a baffling mosaic of candid and crude domestic scenes.
>
> There are shots of a creaky old woman, a harassed mother, her lively little girl and a cheerful husband and father who plainly cannot provide for his small brood. There are scenes, as familiar as next-door neighbours, of the mother trying to get the child to eat, washing clothes, quarrelling with the husband or pushing the child towards school.
>
> Satyajit Ray, Indian artist, who wrote the screenplay and directed this film, provides ample indication that this is his

first professional motion picture job. Any picture as loose in structure or as listless in tempo as this one is would barely pass as a 'rough cut' with the editors in Hollywood.

But, oddly enough, as it continues – as the bits in the mosaic increase and a couple of basically human and dramatic incidents are dropped in, such as the pitiful death of the old woman and the sickness and death of the little girl – the poignant theme emerges and the whole thing takes a slim poetic form. By the time it comes to its sad end, it has the substance of a tender threnody.

Much of the effect is accomplished by some stunningly composed domestic scenes, well performed – or pictured – by an excellent Indian cast, and exquisitely photographed by Subrata Mitra in tastefully filtered blacks and whites. And a finely conceived and sympathetic original musical score, composed by Ravi Shankar, in which native instruments are employed, sets the whole sad story in the frame of a melancholy mood.

Karuna Banerji is touching as the mother who is most distressed by poverty and Uma Das Gupta is lovely and sensitive as the girl. Chunibala Devi is fantastically realistic and effective as the aging crone and Subir Banerji is wistful and beguiling as the small son of the family.

As we say, it is quite exotic. The dialogue often sounds like a Gramophone record going at high speed. English subtitles barely make some sense. But there are lovely little threads in the strange fabric. It's a film that takes patience to be enjoyed.

It was Crowther's habit to publish his further thoughts on a newly released film in the Sunday section of the *New York Times*. On 28 September 1958, he duly wrote again about *Pather Panchali*, as Ray recalled in *Sight and Sound*. In this second review he was compelled to recant his criticism, at least to some extent, such was the hostile public response to his first review. He also now mentioned that the film had received the backing of John Huston in its rough-cut form, four years before its US release. But he could not wholly accept the fact that *Pather Panchali* owed little or nothing to Hollywood, and so could not be judged by Hollywood's criteria for success. Crowther therefore concluded his second review somewhat lamely: 'This is a picture of India of a sort we have not yet had – not even in Jean Renoir's *The River* nor in Robert Flaherty's *Elephant Boy*. This is a communication of human experience out of the heart and fibre of Bengal. It is a universal experience, appropriate to the screens of the world.' Even so, Crowther selected *Pather Panchali* as one of his best foreign films of 1958, and repeated this recommendation in 1959 and 1960, for *Aparajito* and *The World of Apu*, when they were released in New York. In the early 1960s, he became a committed admirer of Ray's films.

Several other US critics felt rather similarly to Crowther, but the majority American verdict was that *Pather Panchali* had, in Ray's much later words, 'irresistible human appeal', whatever its cultural opacities for the West and its technical rough edges. *Time* magazine called it 'perhaps the finest piece of filmed folklore since Robert Flaherty's *Nanook of the North*'; the *New Yorker* spoke of 'a demonstration of what a man can do with a camera and an idea if he really puts his mind to it'; whilst Arlene Croce in *Film Culture* observed: 'I don't know anyone who hasn't seen *Pather Panchali*. ... Whatever else [Ray] may achieve, he has given world cinema one of its monuments.'

The association of Ray with Flaherty by some critics – first stated by Lotte Eisner in her Cannes Festival diary – both helped the commercial success of *Pather Panchali* and hindered its artistic appreciation in the United States. In the opinion of the historian Chandak Sengoopta, 'reviewer after reviewer imagined it to be a Flahertyesque chronicle of real life in rural India' – with the parts presumably played by genuine villagers, rather than actors from the city – despite the fact that this was 'largely an illusion'. (Hence, probably, Crowther's doubt in his review about whether the film was 'performed' or 'pictured' by its cast.) But as rapidly became obvious, when the second and third parts of the trilogy appeared in the United States, the Flaherty tradition had little or nothing to do with Ray's work. Indeed Ray wrote practically nothing about Flaherty, and hardly mentioned his documentaries during my many hours of conversations with him.

Some of those US critics who had waxed ecstatic about the first film, such as Croce, found its sequels to be more conventional and less exciting. Reviewing *The World of Apu*, she wrote: 'he is still a poet, and an exceptionally sensitive one, but his best energies have gone into transcending the dramatic conceptions of his script rather than in embodying them.' This feeling of disappointment with Ray's gradual abandonment of lyricism would lose him many of his early admirers after the early 1960s. But the most perceptive American critical response came from Paul Beckley writing in the *New York Herald Tribune* in 1960 about *The World of Apu*: 'The connoisseur must feel a kind of glow of surprised enthusiasm at the endless rightness of Ray's effects. If they seem in the beginning merely happy, the endless aptness soon makes clear that chance could have little place in the making of a work so beautifully controlled. Yet it is not entirely adequate to speak of control, rather a sort of constancy of inspiration.'

The director Martin Scorsese, then a teenager, remarked of that hopeful period in the cinema when directors such as Ray, Kurosawa, Ingmar Bergman, Federico Fellini, Godard, Truffaut and Andrzej Wajda were at the height of their creative powers:

> One of the great cinematic experiences of my life was in the very early sixties when I watched the complete Apu Trilogy in a New York theatre ... I was as totally absorbed as one would be reading a great epic novel. Satyajit Ray's ability to turn the

> particular into the universal was a revelation to me. I was 18 or 19 years old and had grown up in a very parochial society of Italian-Americans and yet I was deeply moved by what Ray showed of people so far from my own experience. I was moved by how their society and their way of life echoed the same chords in all of us. I then sought out other Ray films like *Devi*, *The Music Room*, *Two Daughters*, and later *Distant Thunder*.
>
> I was very taken by the style of these films – at first so much like the Italian neo-realist films, yet surprising the viewer with bursts of sheer poetry. Ray's use of music impressed me so much that I sought out and eventually found soundtracks to his films, such as Ravi Shankar's music from *Pather Panchali*. Ray's magic, the simple poetry of his images and their emotional impact will always stay with me.

On his first visit to the United States in 1958, Ray met a number of established American directors and writers. In New York he had long chats with Elia Kazan, Paddy Chayevsky and Sidney Lumet, and in Hollywood talked to Stanley Kubrick, George Stevens and Billy Wilder, who was then shooting *Some Like It Hot*. 'You won a prize at Cannes?' was Wilder's opening shot to Ray. 'Well, I guess you're an artist. But I'm not. I'm just a commercial man, and I like it that way.' While visiting all the major studios, he became 'absolutely terrified by the plethora of equipment and personnel', despite the forewarning impression he had received from Renoir in 1949. Two aspects of his trip particularly lodged in his mind: there were no 'poets' among the directors he met, and virtually no one had more than 'the vaguest notions about India'. An MGM executive he lunched with in the studio's basement cafeteria proudly confided to him his casting for a film about the Buddha – Robert Taylor! As Ray remarked soberly in a letter to the Sri Lankan director Lester James Peries in December 1958, after he got back home to Calcutta: 'One realises what the Indian film-maker is up against

– a colossal ignorance and only a moderate inquisitiveness. It is a miracle that *Pather Panchali* is doing so well at the box office. The notions about Japan are equally nebulous, and this airing of ideas about *Kabuki* etc., is just sheer pretence. The East is still as far away from the West as it has ever been...'

Ray on location near Calcutta, 1956, during the making of *Aparajito*

9

Apu in the East and West: The Trilogy and Ray Today

Although Satyajit Ray made more than 30 feature films, his Apu Trilogy, and *Pather Panchali* in particular, remains his most famous work – in Bengal, in India as a whole and in the rest of the world. The Apu Trilogy is the most regularly revived of his films, and by far the best selling on DVD. When Hollywood – nudged by Martin Scorsese and the producer Ismail Merchant – gave Ray an Academy Award for his lifetime achievement as a film-maker, just before his death, *Pather Panchali* was the chief focus of attention in Audrey Hepburn's Oscar presentation ceremony. As the writer Arthur C. Clarke, who knew Ray personally, remarked on the occasion of Ray's 70th birthday in 1991: 'I must admit I get rather restive when people write saying that my first published story was my best: perhaps Satyajit feels the same about his own first-born. But surely *Pather Panchali* is one of the most heart-breakingly beautiful films ever made; there are scenes which I need never view again, because they are burnt into my memory.'

In the course of researching my biography of Ray in the 1980s, I asked him about this situation. 'There's no question that *Pather*

Panchali is still my most popular film in India,' he agreed. 'It's a phenomenon that never ceases to surprise me.' He could not really explain why. When pressed, he said with a slightly irritated laugh: 'I think by and large Bengalis love to have a good cry and this is a film which gives it to them.' Ray always disliked Bengali sentimentality, and its near-companions hard-heartedness and hypocrisy.

Pather Panchali's fame outside India has long disturbed many prosperous Indians (especially in Bollywood), because of the film's depiction of poverty, on which Bosley Crowther focused in his notorious *New York Times* review. Only through Nehru's personal intervention, as we know, did Ray's maiden venture reach the Cannes Film Festival in 1956, and thereby establish India on the map of world cinema.

A quarter of a century later, the very same official objection to the film was raised in the Indian Parliament, this time by Nargis Dutt, MP, the attractive heroine of the 1957 blockbuster *Mother India* (Bollywood's answer to *Pather Panchali*) and one of the biggest box-office stars of her time. Dutt publicly accused Ray of distorting India's image abroad – first in a parliamentary debate, and then in a magazine interview that was symptomatic of Ray's long-running difficulties with his Indian audience outside Bengal:

Interviewer: What does Ray portray in the Apu Trilogy and why do you object to it?

Dutt: He portrays a region of West Bengal which is so poor that it does not represent India's poverty in its true form. Tell me something. Which part of India are you from?

Interviewer: UP [Uttar Pradesh].

Dutt: Now, tell me, would you leave your 80-year-old grandmother to die in a cremation ground, unattended?

Interviewer: No.

Dutt: Well, people in West Bengal do. And that is what he portrays in these films. It is not a correct image of India.

Interviewer: Do people in West Bengal do such a thing?

Dutt: I don't know. But when I go abroad, foreigners ask me embarrassing questions like 'Do you have schools in India?' 'Do you have cars in India?' I feel so ashamed, my eyes are lowered before them. If a foreigner asks me, 'What kind of houses do you live in?', I feel like answering: 'We live on treetops.' Why do you think films like *Pather Panchali* become so popular abroad?

Interviewer: You tell me.

Dutt: Because people there want to see India in an abject condition. That is the image they have of our country and a film that confirms that image seems to them authentic.

Interviewer: But why should a renowned director like Ray do such a thing?

Dutt: To win awards. His films are not commercially successful. They only win awards.

Interviewer: What do you expect Ray to do?

Dutt: What I want is that if Mr Ray projects Indian poverty abroad, he should also show 'Modern India'.

Interviewer: But if the theme and plot of *Pather Panchali* are complete within the realm of a poor village, how can he deliberately fit 'Modern India' in it?

Dutt: But Mr Ray can make separate films on 'Modern India'.

Interviewer: What is 'Modern India'?

Dutt: Dams...

Interviewer: Can you give me one example of a film that portrays 'Modern India'?

Dutt: Well... I can't give you an example offhand...

Ray did not bother to refute such stuff, but others jumped to his defence including the actor and theatre director Utpal Dutta, who joked that 'this holy cow should have stuck to her *Mother India* role', and the Forum for Better Cinema – a group of respected film-makers and writers – who wrote to Nargis Dutt as follows:

> The Modern India you speak of is the India of dams, of scientists, steel plants and agricultural reforms. Do you honestly believe that it is this India that is portrayed in the so-called commercial films of Bombay? In fact, the world of commercial Hindi films is peopled by thugs, smugglers, dacoits, voyeurs, murderers, cabaret dancers, sexual perverts, degenerates, delinquents and rapists, which can hardly be called representative of Modern India.

It was soon after this debate in 1981 that the Government in New Delhi informed Ray it could not grant him permission to make a film about child labour since this did not constitutionally exist in India. So instead, as a deliberate protest against both the ban and the minister concerned (whom Ray openly described as 'a very dangerous, vicious type of person'), he decided to produce *Deliverance/Sadgati* – a film about a helpless low-caste labourer and a ruthless Brahmin priest as bluntly prosaic about grinding poverty and the human condition as *Pather Panchali* is poetically hopeful.

The rapid expansion of the Indian economy since the mid-1990s, and the consequent spurt in affluence and self-confidence of India's middle classes – if scarcely of India's labouring poor – have almost eliminated the earlier official objections to showing Indian poverty in films seen abroad. In 2009, the film *Slumdog Millionaire* (British-made, but based on a novel by an Indian), which revels luridly in the desperate slum poverty of Bombay, won massive audiences outside India along with a fistful of Oscars. There was much rejoicing within India, comparatively little protest, and no mention of the controversy over *Pather Panchali*. Unlike Ray and his Apu, the director of *Slumdog Millionaire*, Danny Boyle, shrewdly set his money-minded young protagonist in 'Modern India', with a cast of thugs, smugglers, murderers, perverts and degenerates sufficient to keep audiences everywhere eagerly watching, helped along by a thumping musical score and a Bollywood-style song-and-dance finale.

Faced with such a crass and exploitative film about India, and its numerous Bollywood equivalents, it is worth reflecting on the views of one of the Bombay film industry's more sensitive figures, the Urdu poet, scriptwriter and hugely successful songwriter Javed Akhtar, who began his film career in the early 1970s. Delivering the Satyajit Ray memorial lecture in Calcutta in 2009, Akhtar expressed his feeling of discouragement with modern Indian movies: 'In a way, they mirror the fact that we are not ready to stop and think. Everybody is in a hurry and is looking for instant gratification without caring for those around them. We are making films that sell this lifestyle to a small, affluent, multiplex-going audience that doesn't bother about the small town and rural population. Ray's films depicted a compassion, a sensitivity that is sadly missing not just from films, but from our lives as well.' Referring to Ray's well-known lack of villains, even in so bleak a film as *The Middle Man/Jana Aranya* about out-and-out corruption, Akhtar remarked: 'His characters only had negative shades. They were people trapped in their own thinking and beliefs. While Hindi films had ferocious villains who only evoked hatred, you actually felt sad for Ray's negative characters. Such was the sensitivity of the man.' He concluded: 'We are trying to hide our own inadequacies that have resulted from a skewed education system. It has not trained us to appreciate our own culture and tradition. Vernacular education [i.e. education in Indian languages, rather than English], on the other hand, has somewhat isolated us from the world. We need to take a long, hard look at ourselves. Or else, we shall continue to feel incomplete and fail to appreciate the subtlety that Ray's films depicted.'

Ironically, the novelist Salman Rushdie provides a good example of Akhtar's concerns. As is well known, Rushdie is a writer fascinated with the subtleties of multicultural identity (for example, in his novel *Midnight's Children*), who was born in Bombay and educated first in that city in an English-medium school and then at British institutions. Writing about Ray and *Pather Panchali* in 1990, Rushdie began his essay with a personal homage to the film:

> 'I can never forget the excitement in my mind after seeing it,' Akira Kurosawa said about Satyajit Ray's first film, *Pather Panchali* (*The Song of the Little Road*), and it's true: this movie, made for next to nothing, mostly with untrained actors, by a director who was learning (and making up) the rules as he went along, is a work of such lyrical and emotional force that it becomes, for its audiences, as potent as their own, most deeply personal memories. To this day, the briefest snatch of Ravi Shankar's wonderful theme music brings back a flood of feeling, and a crowd of images: the single eye of the little Apu, seen at the moment of waking, full of mischief and life; the insects dancing on the surface of the pond, prefiguring the coming monsoon rains; and above all the immortal scene, one of the most tragic in all cinema, in which Harihar the peasant comes home to the village from the city, bringing presents for his children, not knowing that his daughter has died in his absence. When he shows his wife, Sarbajaya, the sari he has brought for the dead girl, she begins to weep; and now he understands, and cries out, too; but (and this is the stroke of genius) their voices are replaced by the high, high music of a single *tarshehnai*, a sound like a scream of the soul.

'Harihar the peasant', writes Rushdie casually. But Harihar is no peasant: he is a Brahmin, a priest, a scholar and a writer, for heaven's sake, who has never touched a plough in his life. An

Indian villager less of a peasant than Harihar would be hard to imagine. 'Harihar Ray was a Brahmin' is the first line of the novel *Pather Panchali* in its English translation, as we know; and in the film Ray makes the character's Brahmin identity abundantly obvious – for a start, priests must be Brahmins in Hinduism – whilst also showing his love of manuscripts and writing, which he shares with his son Apu. Although some western critics have fallen into the same trap as Rushdie, instinctively assuming that only peasants could live in the village poverty shown in *Pather Panchali*, this is no explanation for a writer who prides himself on his Indian origin. It seems that only Rushdie's citified, anglicised education in cosmopolitan Bombay, far away from India's villages and from Bengal, can explain such an error, which remained uncorrected in Rushdie's later collection of his essays, *Imaginary Homelands*.

Rushdie's misunderstanding suggests that Crowther's incomprehension of *Pather Panchali* articulated in the *New York Times* in 1958 is still widespread, despite the film's avowed status as a classic. For instance, when it was revived in London in August 2005, on the 50th anniversary of its first release, *Pather Panchali* received a brief review from James Christopher, the chief film critic of the London *Times*. Although *The Times* had a tradition of intelligently reviewing and discussing Ray's work that went back to the 1950s, notably under its former chief film critic David Robinson, its 2005 review was arrogant and inane. Judge for yourself:

> Satyajit Ray's Apu Trilogy follows the life of a poor village boy from slum to city. The first film, *Pather Panchali* (1955), was a blast from the heart, and the first reel to make a serious impression in the West with its blistering portrait of a Brahmin family in the grip of poverty.
>
> Not a lot happens in their sweltering Bengalese hamlet. The father, with potty dreams of becoming a playwright, slopes off to distant towns to earn his fortune. His stony wife is left

> fending for two young children and an ancient aunt blessed with a stoop, a squint, and thieving hands.
>
> The walking pace laces the poison. Ray's slow-shutter snapshots of India's shift from a rural to an urban society make up one of the great documents of 20th-century cinema.

Inaccurate or inappropriate words and phrases such as 'slum', 'blast', 'blistering', 'sweltering', 'slopes off', 'earn his fortune', 'stony', 'thieving', 'poison', 'slow-shutter snapshots' and 'document' (shades of Flaherty) – not to mention 'Bengalese', which does not appear in the dictionary – show that the critic has totally misunderstood the setting, characters and mood of the film. Nor does he get around to mentioning Apu by name as one of the two children, despite Apu's central role in the trilogy. No wonder that Christopher finds little happening and the pace plodding – he clearly cannot be bothered to look seriously at the film, because poverty, India and everyday behaviour are not what matter to him in movies, unless they are glamourised and translated into a recognisably Hollywoodish idiom, such as *Slumdog Millionaire* (which Christopher admired).

It is instructive to compare this review with Pauline Kael's equally short review of *Pather Panchali*, republished in the *New Yorker* – another publication with a long-standing interest in Ray's films – at the time of the film's anniversary in August 2005:

> This first film by the masterly Satyajit Ray – possibly the most unembarrassed of directors – is a quiet reverie about the life of an impoverished Brahmin family in a Bengali village. Beautiful, sometimes funny, and full of love, it brought a new vision of India to the screen. Though the central characters are the boy Apu (who is born near the beginning) and his mother and father and sister, the character who makes the strongest impression on you may be the ancient, parasitic, storytelling relative, played by the 80-year-old Chunibala

Devi, a performer who apparently enjoyed coming back into the limelight after 30 years of obscurity – her wages paid for the narcotics she used daily. As 'Auntie', she is so remarkably likeable that you may find the relationship between her and the mother, who is trying to feed her children and worries about how much the old lady eats, very painful. In Bengali.

So dissimilar are these two reviews, that they appear to be describing two different films.

Ray was certainly grateful for sensitive western appreciation such as Kael's (and that of many others, starting with the critics at the Cannes Festival in 1956), and was resigned to the fact that some western critics would not bother with his films or would patronise them with faint praise – from *Pather Panchali* right up to the end of his career in 1992. 'But why should the West care?' he reasonably asked in an article in 1963. Two decades later, he said: 'The cultural gap between East and West is too wide for a handful of films to reduce it. It can happen only when critics back it up with study on other levels as well. But where is the time, with so many other films from other countries to contend with? And where is the compulsion?'

Rather than rely on the loyalty of his foreign audience, Ray preferred to follow his instinct and make films primarily for Bengalis. He was never able to predict which of his films would do well abroad anyway – the success of *The Music Room* came as a real surprise to him, for instance – and so he generally aimed to make his films pay their way in Bengal alone (with the exception of *The Chess Players*). 'It is better not to spend too much rather than to find ways to be sure of the return,' as he explained. In the majority of cases the sums worked out and foreign sales simply added to the profit in Bengal. 'Whatever comes from abroad is extra,' Ray said.

It is an interesting question whether Ray would have been able to survive had he been obliged to operate in a western environment from the beginning, though as with most such hypotheses the premise is suspect: Ray abstracted from Bengal could not have been the individual he was. The film-maker Lindsay Anderson considered that probably he would not have lasted very long, if one was thinking of 'someone who sets himself the standards of quality and refinement and seriousness and artistry Satyajit does, and who lives by them and wouldn't think of giving them up, and does not make films according to any popular conception of entertainment.' Anderson maintained that Ray's position compared with western directors was both very much tougher – technically speaking – and also easier – economically speaking – because it cost so much less to make a film in Calcutta than it did in the West, as witness *Pather Panchali*.

He may have been right, although Anderson perhaps underestimated the perquisites of genius in any setting. There seems no reason in principle why a western Ray should not have been able to gather round him the loyal actors and co-workers that an Ingmar Bergman, or even a Woody Allen, did. But certainly one cannot imagine Ray working as part of any large organisation. Perhaps for him it was a case of once bitten (by the West Bengal Government) on his first film, twice shy. He was courted many times, by the Hollywood producer David Selznick at one extreme to the BBC at the other – whom he eventually declined, in 1978, for the revealing reason that he 'found himself temperamentally unsuited to working for a sponsor – however liberal.'

He may have had his brush with Selznick in mind when he made that remark. It took place in Berlin in 1964 after Ray had won the Selznick Golden Laurel three times at the Berlin Film Festival (for *Pather Panchali*, *Aparajito* and *Two Daughters*). This time Ray had agreed to present the award to Bergman for *Winter Light*. On the day itself he and Selznick had lunch together and Selznick asked him to make a film for him. Ray told him he knew about his famous memos to directors and said he doubted whether he could put up with them. Selznick protested: 'No! With you it'll be different, because, you know, John Huston used to come drunk on the set, so I had to be careful with him, I had to control him, so I sent memos.' Ray said he would think about it. That evening, before the award ceremony, he found a little envelope waiting for him at his hotel. 'In it was a memo from Mr Selznick,' recalled Ray, 'outlining the speech that I was supposed to make, saying would I memorise the six- or seven-line speech that he had written. Well, I made a different speech. It virtually amounted to the same thing because all you had to do was lead up to the name, which was a *great* secret. There are a hundred different ways of doing that, so I chose my way of doing it – not Mr Selznick's way. After that, of course, he didn't write to me again.'

The other important aspect of Ray that Anderson left out of his reckoning in imagining him transplanted to foreign soil, was his popularity with his home audience. Ray was as successful as Bergman was in Sweden, or Kurosawa in Japan, perhaps more so. He hit an all-time high in Bengal with *The Adventures of Goopy and Bagha* in 1968, but there was barely a film he made that did not have an appeal well beyond the confines of a highbrow audience – including, of course, the Apu Trilogy. Without artifice he packed his films with layers of meaning that pleased everyone in different ways, from university professors who normally despised Indian cinema to sentimental housewives brought up on songs and dances in movies and even the better-educated members of Calcutta's vast working class. No one else in Indian cinema has been able to pull off this feat with more than the occasional film, although the fact is not widely appreciated in India outside the Bengali-speaking region. The Bollywood film-maker's view of him was probably summarised by Ramesh Sippy, the maker of the blockbuster *Sholay*, who in 1983 said: 'I always regard Ray as the first moderniser of the Indian cinema and its first artist. The level to which he goes in probing his characters is beyond the reach of an ordinary viewer ... Ray will never be able to make a film for the masses. His attitude to cinema is different. In our country nobody, not even Ray, has tried to bridge the gulf between art and entertainment.'

Although it is true that the all-India television series *Satyajit Ray Presents* (directed by Ray's son Sandip Ray in the 1980s, from scripts by his father) subsequently helped to make Ray's work better known in India outside Bengal, he remained essentially 'only a name' there – by his own admission. Apart from Bangalore, which turned out a good audience for Ray because of its high proportion of professional residents, his films were generally shown in India's major cities in Bengali only – at most, with English subtitles – and at special screenings, usually on Sunday mornings. They were never released nationwide and, apart from *Kapurush/The Coward*, were not dubbed into Hindi. (Subtitles would not have helped since many Hindi-speakers were illiterate.)

In Bengal, Ray sat on the 'Olympian heights', as he once ironically put it – at least by comparison with Bombay. The release of a new film by Ray in Calcutta had long been an event – ever since the furore around *Pather Panchali* in 1955 – which triggered a torrent of reviews and comments in the Bengali and English-language press. While Calcutta's intellectuals – self-styled and otherwise – liked to view a Satyajit Ray film 'with a Satyajit Ray mind' (to quote Ray's actress relative Ruma Guha Thakurta), other people would pass whispered remarks in the auditorium about his more daring challenges to middle-class convention. Sometimes he lost his audience with his cinematic sophistication – as in *Kanchenjungha*, *Days and Nights in the Forest* and *Branches of the Tree/Sakha Prasakha*; occasionally he offended them – as with Apu's harsh treatment of his mother in *Aparajito*; but usually he strongly engaged them in the best traditions of popular art. As he once said, 'Popular taste has produced Greek Drama, Shakespeare, *The Magic Flute,* Chaplin and the Western. ... I do not know of a single film-maker who has been dismayed by a wide acceptance of his work.'

But he was never under any illusions about the difficulties he faced. When he began, in the early 1950s, his audience knew 'tame, torpid versions of popular Bengali novels'; they had been 'reduced to a state of unredeemable vacuity by years of cinematic spoon-feeding'. By the 1980s, not much had changed. 'You'll find directors here so backward, so stupid, and so trashy that you'll find it difficult to believe their works exist alongside my films', said Ray. Very often he and they were shooting in adjacent studios in Calcutta; it was eye-opening to leave his set and sample the typical Bengali cinematic fare. From time to time Ray had bouts of cynicism about his audience – he knew too well that what most of them really wanted was 'a good cry' (which *Pather Panchali* never ceased to deliver) – but he continued to believe that he could educate them and that there had been a slow improvement in their capacity to appreciate good work. This belief, together with the appreciation of foreign audiences, was what sustained him in his early years, and what he chose to pass on in a tough convocation address to the Class of 1974 about to leave India's Film and Television Institute at Pune: 'No matter how you make your film, if you are truly gifted, you will sooner or later create your own market. If not, and you still want to stay in business, then the only rules you would be obliged to follow would be the rules of compromise.'

He was less sanguine about educating the critics in India, 'which, in films, means anybody with access to print'. When he was starting out, 'what passed for film criticism in India usually consisted of a tortuous recounting of a film's plot, followed by a random dispersal of praise or blame on the people concerned in its making. Neither the film-makers nor the public took much heed of it', he wrote in 1982. Although he accepted that it had improved, partly as a result of the film society movement and its writings, Ray maintained that his critics – at least in Bengal – did not affect his work in any way. Since most of them still believed *Pather Panchali* to be his best film, he pointed out sardonically – how could they claim to have improved his films?

In general, he recognised the role of the film critic as a connoisseur: someone who can interpret original work for the benefit of an audience who may otherwise dismiss it. He valued critiques of his own work (even Crowther on *Pather Panchali*) when they coincided with his own estimation of its strengths and weaknesses, but he felt that few who wrote about films – whether Indians or westerners – were properly equipped to do it; when they were, he suspected they would have preferred to become film-makers themselves, like the *Cahiers du Cinéma* critics in France, Lindsay Anderson in Britain, and himself in India. Reading the total volume of critical writing about him since 1955, one can understand Ray's scepticism. Laudatory though much of it is – often amounting to a 'rave' – it seldom rises to the demands of its subject. 'What is attempted in most films of mine is, of course, a synthesis', wrote Ray in *Sight and Sound* in 1982. 'But it can be seen as such only by someone who has his feet in both cultures' – East and West. 'Someone who will bring to bear on the films involvement and detachment in equal measure. Someone who will see both the wood and the trees.' The problem is, neither the Bengali nor the western critics of his films share their creator's easy familiarity with East and West (as described in chapter 1). Bengali critics are too close to and too involved with the stories, while western audiences are too distant and too detached from them.

* * *

What is the future of Ray's artistic legacy? In 1989, he wrote: 'I am sure Chaplin's name will survive even if the cinema ceases to exist as a medium of artistic expression. Chaplin is truly immortal.' What about Ray's name? Is it likely to be immortal? I should say yes – but only as long as the cinema continues to exist as a means of artistic expression. Among people who take films seriously, rather than chiefly as entertainment, the best of Ray's work will be watched, along with the works of Chaplin, Bergman, Eisenstein,

Fellini, Ford, Hitchcock, Kurosawa, Ozu, Renoir, Welles and maybe a few other directors like Scorsese (no other Indians).

The Nobel laureate V. S. Naipaul, a great and many-faceted twentieth-century writer, said truly of Ray (and Kurosawa): 'They are not, like the Americans, looking for a property. They are doing on film what the old novelists of the nineteenth century did. They are describing their societies, their cultures, in the modern medium. Their work hangs together; it's about their view of the world, being given in different ways at different times.'

But this begs a question: how much will the twenty-first century care about the society and culture Ray's films describe? Indian culture in the broad sense will surely continue to be important, like the cultures of America, Europe, Russia, the Arab world, China and Japan – but Ray's films have always had a strained relationship with the India beyond Bengal, and a non-existent one with the world of Bollywood. A few of the leading Indian film-makers outside Bengal do acknowledge a debt to Ray; but it seems heartfelt only in the case of Adoor Gopalakrishnan.

What of the specifically Bengali culture to which Ray repeatedly said he really belonged? Here it is difficult to be sanguine. The widespread indifference of many American and European reviewers to Ray's films, particularly the later films, stems, ultimately, from western indifference to Bengali culture. This did not matter so much with the lyrical *Pather Panchali* but impinged somewhat on *Aparajito*, more on *The World of Apu*, and became an obstacle to wide appreciation of the films Ray made from the mid-1960s onwards. Generally speaking, the more Ray's characters talked about Bengali culture, the less interested in them foreign critics were. (For example, the *Financial Times* critic Nigel Andrews on Ray's brilliant final film, *The Stranger*: 'Like all Ray's late films, it features characters stuck as if by superglue to the ancestral armchairs. Occasionally, stiffly, they rise to walk about the room. And always they talk.')

As for the Bengali audience, the cosmopolitanism for which Bengal was once famous has been largely replaced by that parochialism of outlook – the *kupamanduk* ('frog in the well') tendency passingly referred to in *Aparajito* and lambasted in *The Stranger*. 'We may live in a remote corner of Bengal,' the headmaster tells the teenage Apu, 'but that does not mean our outlook should be narrow.' 'Don't you have any ambition?' a college friend asks Apu in Calcutta. 'You'll just go on living here like the frog in the well? You won't go abroad even if you have the chance?' The best of the current Bengali film-makers, notably Gautam Ghosh, Rituparno Ghosh and Aparna Sen, take serious note of Ray's films; but most Bengalis, frankly speaking, are not serious about them – so much so that there was negligible Calcutta press coverage of the first ever complete retrospective of Ray's films, shown at the National Film Theatre in London in 2002; an indifference unthinkable when Ray was in mid-career.

In my view, there is a definite risk that Ray's work, except for the Apu Trilogy, will become trapped in a cultural eddy by the very breadth and uniqueness of its creator's range of eastern and western references: neither in the mainstream of world cinema like Kurosawa's films, nor in the Bengali backwaters like his contemporary Ritwik Ghatak's.

I hope not. Speaking for myself, I know I shall continue to revisit Ray's films as I do favourite novels, paintings and music. Especially the Apu Trilogy, *The Music Room*, *The Goddess*, *The Postmaster*, *Charulata*, *The Adventures of Goopy and Bagha*, *Days and Nights in the Forest*, *The Adversary*, *The Chess Players*, *Pikoo*, *Branches of the Tree* and *The Stranger*. Almost half of his total work as a film-maker. What more can one ask from a creative genius?

Epilogue
Ray Talks about the Apu Trilogy

This discussion between Satyajit Ray and the author is taken from interviews that took place at various times in the 1980s, during the research for my biography *Satyajit Ray: The Inner Eye*. It is intended to give a general impression of Ray's ideas and personality, rather than to cover all of the important aspects of the Apu Trilogy that are discussed in the main text. His own delightful account of the making of *Pather Panchali* was published as an article, 'A long time on the little road', in *Sight and Sound*, in 1957, and appears in his collection of articles, *Our Films Their Films*.

AR: I have a feeling *Pather Panchali* is still your most popular film in India?

SR: There's no question. It's a phenomenon that never ceases to surprise me.

AR: Why do you think that is?

SR: I don't know. New generations coming up. And Calcutta being such a populous city – there are still obviously lots of people left who haven't seen the film.

AR: Is there an element of nostalgia creeping in? All the changes of the past 30 years?

SR: Well, the change is not so apparent in a village as in a city. If it had been a city story, like *Apur Sansar*, which doesn't have traffic jams, population growth and so on...

AR: But couldn't it be a longing for a simple life?

SR: Possibly, but I think by and large Bengalis love to have a good cry and this is a film which gives it to them.

AR: Do you regard the Apu Trilogy as period films?

SR: To a certain extent yes. Apu in *Aparajito* is dressed in the 1930s fashion. Period in the sense of the 1920s to the end of the 1930s – between the wars. I merely stuck to that period because Bibhutibhusan [Banerji] wrote the novel around 1931. It was contemporary then; the final part was contemporary anyway. I preferred to stick to that period. Certain rituals shown in the film, and the way Apu gets married – all that set it in a slightly earlier period than now. People would then accept such things. Marriages like that may still happen in remote villages and small towns occasionally; they are certainly not something very common now. But that is what would happen if orthodoxy were being observed. The way Apu is married is definitely an orthodox custom.

AR: In India, a critic wrote recently that when you see *Pather Panchali* you feel that you know what it is like to be absolutely poor. Did you feel that you were able to make that kind of adjustment when you were making it?

SR: I was helped by the book. In those days I had no confidence as a dialogue writer. Most of the dialogue comes directly from the book, word for word, because I felt that I could rely totally on Bibhuti Banerji. He belonged so much to that milieu. I think my contribution comes in the poetic elements in the film, all the ideas which came: the scene of watching the train, the death of the old woman, the wife crying when the husband arrives and the music taking the place of the scream – that was all my contribution. But the rest of it – the mood of the film, and what it means – all that comes from the author. I felt very, very sympathetic to the whole thing. Of course, I had no idea of village life, but fortunately villages were just outside the city limits at that time. Boral, the location of *Pather Panchali*, was only about seven miles from my house. Now that place is hardly recognisable – it's been electrified, big houses have come up, roads have been metalled – but when the film was shot, you had an authentic village just outside the city. And we used to go there before we started shooting. In fact, it was a habit of my art director Bansi Chandragupta and I – it was our Sunday outing – to take a train and go to a village and spend the day looking and absorbing.

AR: What were you looking for in the location?

SR: I went to the village of the story, the author's village. It was unsuitable because it was not photogenic enough. I was looking for certain elements, it's very difficult to say which, but they strike you.

AR: There must have been an element of compromise even in your final choice?

SR: Yes. Take the field of *kash* where the children discover the train. That was far away from our location and there was no river, which is in the story. So I just dropped the river from the film. But the pond was right next to the house and that was an important element.

AR: How did you set about getting to know the people in the village where you shot?

SR: I owe this to a friend of ours, one of the six or seven founders of the Calcutta Film Society – Manoj Majumdar. He had a relation who had a house in Boral, and Manoj knew the village very well. He suggested we should take a look at it because it was close to Calcutta. We hadn't even heard of Boral. We had heard of Garia, on the left side of the main road. Boral was on the right. Manoj took us by car to Boral and introduced us to his family and we took a look around and we happened upon this ramshackle old house by the pond. To begin with the people were not particularly friendly. They didn't like the idea of a film, with people arriving. The young people were very excited, however. Nobody had heard of me or of any of the actors except for Kanu Banerji. We saw the house. We discussed among ourselves if this might do, if Bansi was able to do things to it like reconstructing it and removing all its undergrowth. I was particularly struck by the pond and the house, and the surroundings were fairly quiet. Once we'd found the house, we had to find the owner of the house, who was living in Kalighat. So we met the owner in Calcutta and he was a nasty old man coming out with four-letter words all the time, bed-ridden. He said we'd have to pay him 50 rupees a month. That was the rent that we paid every month for two and a half years to this man. The house was completely ruined and we had a really tough job of reconstructing the whole thing, cleaning it up, building a compound wall and fixing doors to it. We built a kitchen. The old woman's house was already there: the little cottage. By that time, of course, we had got to know the village people quite well.

AR: Who was your first choice of cameraman?

SR: Nemai Ghosh, I think. I don't recall this, but Subrata [Mitra] has mentioned this in several interviews, with himself as assistant to Nemai Ghosh. I definitely recall sending for Subrata and announcing that I had decided to make him the cameraman. At the same time I told him that if you've done still photography, you know your exposures, it's not as difficult as they make it sound.

AR: Did Cartier-Bresson's photographs help you?

SR: His available light attitude to photography, yes. I don't think a still photographer really influences a *film* to that extent, but Cartier-Bresson's feeling for light, the fact that he never used flashes ... We decided that we would not be using the Hollywood style of photography, which goes for the use of lots of big lights and a kind of artificial kind of look. It was the spontaneous quality of Cartier-Bresson's photography, and the fact that he was using available light as far as possible, occasionally using reflectors to boost the shadows. That is unavoidable. Otherwise you have extreme contrasts, which is not very pleasing. But using reflectors in a way that people would not be conscious of. *Pather Panchali* was largely confined to day scenes shot on location – of course, the night scenes had nothing to do with Cartier-Bresson.

AR: With all the obstacles, how did you keep up your morale while making the film?

SR: I think I was pretty confident that I was doing something fairly important – certainly from the point of view of Indian films. I didn't yet think in terms of world cinema, or making a mark internationally. But definitely I was convinced that this was going to be a milestone in Indian films. Because I was using methods which nobody had used before and they were proving successful. The rushes told us that. The rushes told us that the children were behaving marvellously and the old woman was an absolute stunner. Nobody had ever seen such an old woman in an Indian film before. So this kept me going. There was a big break of a year after we had edited about 4,000 feet of film. In fact, people were told that this is the end. So everyone was very unhappy. But I kept hoping that something would turn up, somebody with some money would come forward. So the morale came from the fact that I was able to keep up my interest in the film because of my confidence in what I had already shot. And I knew that there were many more exciting scenes to come.

AR: When the government took over as producer, you say you had to account to them by instalments. What did that mean?

SR: It meant long delays I'm afraid, and it was very unpleasant. It meant, for one thing, that we missed the rainy season, and we had to shoot the rain scenes in October.

Throughout the rainy season we had no money. It meant going to the location every day with the entire crew and cast and just waiting. There were days and days of waiting and doing nothing when we just sat there ... It was a kind of picnic, but not a very pleasant picnic. We would keep looking at the sky and little patches of cloud, which wouldn't produce any rain. So that became a habit.

AR: Do you think your habit of editing rushes while you are still shooting comes from this time?

SR: Yes, it's become a habit. I think I made it a method of work. Later, at the time of *Charulata*, which was predominantly studio shooting, we would have a set, a fairly elaborate set. The rushes would come, and for the next set we would need at least a fortnight before shooting again. While we waited we had nothing to do, so why not edit? But I would re-edit *Pather Panchali* now. It would improve. The pace sometimes falters, not in the second half though. We shot the film in sequence, and we learnt as we went long and so the second half hangs together much better. But it would definitely improve with cutting. And there are certain things we couldn't do anything about, like camera placements. I don't think the relationship of the three little cottages is very clear in the film. Because you see, in a film, you have to choose a master angle which you have to keep repeating so that people get their bearings. If you keep changing the camera angle, it becomes very confusing. In your mind the plan is very clear but to make it clear on the screen you have to use certain devices which we didn't know at that time.

AR: You learnt that through experience?

SR: Oh yes, *Aparajito* has no such mistakes. There, the editing was rushed. But there are some fine passages of cutting: the death of the father and the pigeons and everything, and Sarbajaya's decision to leave the job with the cut to the train. All of that I found very effective and very well done: exactly as I had conceived them. The longeurs in the film are largely because of the poor soundtrack. If there had been more for the ear to absorb, those scenes wouldn't have seemed so long.

AR: You have said that the flow of ideas is something you can neither account for nor recapture. Do your best ideas come to you quickly – even in a flash?

SR: 'In a flash' is just the expression I would use. For instance, the scene in *Pather Panchali* where Apu throws the necklace into the pond and the scum spreads, then closes in again, I think that's a lovely thing. It happened on a certain day when we were not shooting, just sitting by the pond. The weather had turned bad or something like that and there were pebbles which I was throwing in. Suddenly I noticed this phenomenon happening. In the original novel, Apu just throws the necklace into the bamboo forest, and that was also in my script. Then it struck me how wonderful this would be. It's like that – I jumped up almost at the marvellous idea. ... This whole business of creation, of the ideas that come in a flash, cannot be explained by science. It cannot. I don't know what can explain it but I know that the best ideas come at moments when you're not even thinking of it. It's a very private thing really.

Films Directed by Satyajit Ray

The films are listed by date of release in Bengal, or date of completion if not released. Credits are given only for the Apu Trilogy.

1955
PATHER PANCHALI (THE SONG OF THE LITTLE ROAD)

Producer: Government of West Bengal. Screenplay from the novel *Pather Panchali* by Bibhutibhusan Banerji: Satyajit Ray. Photography: Subrata Mitra. Editor: Dulal Dutta. Art director: Bansi Chandragupta. Music: Ravi Shankar. Sound: Bhupen Ghosh. Running time: 113 minutes.

Cast: Kanu Banerji (*Harihar*), Karuna Banerji (*Sarbajaya*), Subir Banerji (*Apu*), Uma Das Gupta (*Durga*), Chunibala Devi (*Indir Thakrun*), Runki Banerji (*Child Durga*), Reba Devi (*Sejbou*), Aparna Devi (*Nilmoni's wife*), Tulsi Chakravarti (*Prasanna, schoolmaster/grocer*), Binoy Mukherji (*Baidyanath Majumdar, village elder*), Haren Banerji (*Chinibash, sweet-seller*), Harimohan Nag (*Doctor*), Haridhan Nag (*Chakravarti*), Nibhanoni Devi (*Dasi*), Ksirod Roy (*Priest*), Rama Ganguli (*Ranu*).

1956
APARAJITO (THE UNVANQUISHED)

Producer: Epic Films. Screenplay from the novel *Aparajito* by Bibhutibhusan Banerji: Satyajit Ray. Photography: Subrata Mitra. Editor: Dulal Dutta. Art director: Bansi Chandragupta. Music: Ravi Shankar. Sound: Durgadas Mitra. Running time: 113 minutes.

Cast: Kanu Banerji (*Harihar*), Karuna Banerji (*Sarbajaya*), Pinaki Sen Gupta (*Boy Apu*), Smaran Ghosal (*Adolescent Apu*), Santi Gupta (*Lahiri's wife*), Ramani Sen Gupta (*Bhabataran*), Ranibala (*Teli*), Sudipta Roy (*Nirupama*), Ajay Mitra (*Anil*), Charuprakash Ghosh (*Nanda*), Subodh Ganguli (*Headmaster*), Moni Srimani (*Schools inspector*), Hemanta Chatterji (*Professor*), Kali Banerji (*Kathak*), Kalicharan Roy (*Akhil, press proprietor*), Kamala Adhikari (*Moksada*), Lalchand Banerji (*Lahiri*), K. S. Pande (*Pande*), Meenaksi Devi (*Pande's wife*), Anil Mukherji (*Abinash*), Harendrakumar Chakravarti (*Doctor*), Bhaganu Palwan (*Palwan*).

1959
APUR SANSAR (THE WORLD OF APU)

Producer: Satyajit Ray Productions. Screenplay from the novel *Aparajito* by Bibhutibhusan Banerji: Satyajit Ray. Photography: Subrata Mitra. Editor: Dulal Dutta. Art director: Bansi Chandragupta. Music: Ravi Shankar. Sound: Durgadas Mitra. Running time: 106 minutes.

Cast: Soumitra Chatterji (*Apu*), Sharmila Tagore (*Aparna*), Alok Chakravarti (*Kajal*), Swapan Mukherji (*Pulu*), Dhiresh Majumdar (*Sasinarayan, Pulu's uncle*), Sefalika Devi (*Sasinarayan's wife*), Tusar Banerji (*Bridegroom*), Dhiren Ghosh (*Landlord*), Abhijit Chatterji (*Murari*).

By far the best DVD edition of the Apu Trilogy is the three-disc version that was released by Artificial Eye in 2003. The picture and sound have been digitally restored; the subtitles are good, if not perfect; and the extras include my production notes, the 1952 storyboards for *Pather Panchali*, extracts from a BBC Television documentary, *The Cinema of Satyajit Ray* (1988), and finally a complete Channel 4 Television documentary, *Movie Masterclass* (1990), in which the film-maker and producer Mamoun Hassan analyses *The World of Apu* with a group of film students from the UK's National Film and Television School.

1958 PARASH PATHAR (THE PHILOSOPHER'S STONE)
1958 JALSAGHAR (THE MUSIC ROOM)
1960 DEVI (THE GODDESS)
1961 TEEN KANYA (THREE DAUGHTERS)
This film includes The Postmaster, Monihara (The Lost Jewels) and Samapti (The Conclusion).
1961 RABINDRANATH TAGORE (documentary)
1962 KANCHENJUNGHA
1962 ABHIJAN (THE EXPEDITION)
1963 MAHANAGAR (THE BIG CITY)
1964 CHARULATA (THE LONELY WIFE)
1964 TWO
1965 KAPURUSH-O-MAHAPURUSH (THE COWARD AND THE HOLY MAN)
1966 NAYAK (THE HERO)
1967 CHIRIAKHANA (THE ZOO)
1968 GOOPY GYNE BAGHA BYNE (THE ADVENTURES OF GOOPY AND BAGHA)
1969 ARANYER DIN RATRI (DAYS AND NIGHTS IN THE FOREST)
1970 PRATIDWANDI (THE ADVERSARY)
1971 SEEMABADDHA (COMPANY LIMITED)
1971 SIKKIM (documentary)
1972 THE INNER EYE (documentary)
1973 ASANI SANKET (DISTANT THUNDER)

1974	SONAR KELLA (THE GOLDEN FORTRESS)
1975	JANA ARANYA (THE MIDDLE MAN)
1976	BALA (documentary)
1977	SHATRANJ KE KHILARI (THE CHESS PLAYERS)
1978	JOI BABA FELUNATH (THE ELEPHANT GOD)
1980	HIRAK RAJAR DESE (THE KINGDOM OF DIAMONDS)
1980	PIKOO
1981	SADGATI (DELIVERANCE)
1984	GHARE BAIRE (THE HOME AND THE WORLD)
1987	SUKUMAR RAY (documentary)
1989	GANASATRU (AN ENEMY OF THE PEOPLE)
1990	SAKHA PRASAKHA (BRANCHES OF THE TREE)
1991	AGANTUK (THE STRANGER)

References

Quoted interviews with Satyajit Ray, his actors, collaborators, friends and associates were conducted by me and took place at various times between 1982 and 1988 during the research for my biography *Satyajit Ray: The Inner Eye* (2nd edn, London: I.B.Tauris, 2004). Where a full reference for a published source is not given, see the Bibliography for further details.

Chapter 1 Self-taught Film-maker: Satyajit Ray's Formative Years

1: 'I never imagined' Interview with Andrew Robinson
2: 'As material for a film' Ibid.
2: 'My grandfather was a rare combination' Introduction to Sukumar Ray, *The Select Nonsense of Sukumar Ray* (Sukanta Chaudhuri, trans.), Calcutta: Oxford University Press, 1987: unpaginated
2: 'As far as my father's writing and drawing goes' Ibid.
3: 'Even today, if I catch a whiff of turpentine' Ray, *Jakhan Chhoto Chhilam*: 15
4: 'I mean I have no money worries' Interview with Andrew Robinson
4: 'Adults treat all children' Ray, *Jakhan Chhoto Chhilam*: 23
5: 'Loneliness and being alone' Interview with Andrew Robinson
5: 'imbibing' Ibid.
6: 'free bioscope' Ray, *Jakhan Chhoto Chhilam*: 24

6: 'Who knows? Perhaps this was' Ibid.: 26
6: 'weeks of musing on its wonders' Ray, 'My life, my work', pt 1
6: 'an early example of Indian soft porn' Ray, 'I wish I could have shown them to you', *Cinema Vision India*, 1:1 (1980): 6
7: 'Lillian Gish' Ray, *Our Films Their Films*: 129
7: 'a forbidden world … Verdi' Ray, 'My life, my work', pt 1
8: 'We laughed at Jack Hulbert' Ray, *Our Films Their Films*: 143
9: 'perpetually shrouded' Ray, 'Under western eyes': 270
9: 'at an age when the Bengali youth' Ray, 'My life, my work', pt 1
10: 'Erudition is something which I singularly lack' Ibid.
10: 'My relationship with Shantiniketan' Ray, 'My life, my work', pt 2
12: 'a nice fellow but a shockingly bad artist' Letter to Norman Clare, 22 May 1948
12: 'Ray was a man of real integrity' J. B. R. Nicholson: interview with Andrew Robinson
12: 'If you had really thought about what you were doing' Interview with Andrew Robinson
13: 'He interpreted the words in such a way' Subrata Banerji, *Film World*, Bombay, April–May 1971: 33
13: 'The book filled me with admiration' Ray, *My Years with Apu*: 11
15: 'One gets used to everything ultimately' Interview with Andrew Robinson
16: 'although the top line [of the score]' Letter to Norman Clare, 25 Aug. 1990
16: 'I propose to have a room of my own' Letter to Alex Aronson, 19 Sept. 1945
16: 'not nearly as much comfort' Letter to Norman Clare, 22 May 1948
17: 'There was a long time' Interview with Andrew Robinson
17: 'Do not look down upon the *addas*' Benoy Kumar Sarkar, quoted by R. P. Gupta in *Sunday*, Calcutta, 5–11 Jan. 1986

18: 'I am taking the cinema more and more seriously' Letter to Norman Clare, 22 May 1948
18: 'hieroglyphic notes' Ray, *Our Films Their Films*: 49
18: 'This was the film that first' Ray, *My Years with Apu*: 16
18: 'The Gothic gloom of the film' Ray, *Our Films Their Films*: 6
19: 'I never knew Indian music and dancing' Letter to Norman Clare, 22 May 1948
19: 'The raw material of cinema' Ray, *Our Films Their Films*: 24
20: 'He was slightly critical of the way' Interview with Folke Isaksson, *Sight and Sound*, London, summer 1970: 115
20: 'All we had to do was go to Nepal' Interview with Andrew Robinson
20: 'like a pricked balloon ... Hollywoodish' Ray, 'My life, my work', pt 3
21: 'I think what Hollywood really needs' Quoted in Ray, *Our Films Their Films*: 114
21: 'In America, they worry too much' Ibid.: 118
21: 'I think that subconsciously' Interview with Bikram Singh, *Introspections: Satyajit Ray*, India, 1991 (documentary film)
21: 'principal mentor' Speech accepting the Legion of Honour, Calcutta, 2 Feb. 1989
21: 'Doubtless the management' Ray, *Our Films Their Films*: 9
22: 'It was a face-to-face confrontation' Interview with Andrew Robinson
22: 'I had always thought the English in England' Quoted in Seton: 82
23: 'I always knew Satyajit to be intelligent' Interview with Andrew Robinson
23: 'deification ... pressures' Ray, *Our Films Their Films*: 211
23: 'Lindsay was absolutely up in arms' Interview with Andrew Robinson
24: 'I responded to Ford' Ibid.
24: 'gored' Interview with Folke Isaksson, *Sight and Sound*, London, summer 1970: 116
24: 'I came out of the theatre' Ray, 'My life, my work', pt 3

24: 'The entire conventional approach' Quoted in Seton: 165

25: 'Zavattini's greatest assets' Ray, *Our Films Their Films*: 126–27

25: 'the most enchanting, the most impudent and the most sublime' Ray, *Music I Live By*, All India Radio, 1966 (radio talk)

26: 'Venice is a fantastic place' Letter to Bansi Chandragupta, exact date unknown, quoted in Seton: 119

Chapter 2 Apu in Fiction and Film: Adapting the Novels *Pather Panchali* and *Aparajito*

28: 'one of the few completely satisfying Bengali novels' Buddhadeva Bose, *An Acre of Green Grass: A Review of Modern Bengali Literature*, Calcutta: Orient Longmans, 1948: 88

28: 'The boy-hero Apu grows up' Ibid.: 89

30: 'In his novels he showed' Nirad C. Chaudhuri, *The Hand, Great Anarch!: India 1921–1952*, London: Chatto & Windus , 1987: 90

30: 'I saw often that he could be' Ibid.: 95

31: 'The script had to retain' Ray, *Our Films Their Films*: 33

33: 'Durga was a big girl now' Banerji, *Pather Panchali*: 156–57

33: 'You had to find out for yourself' Ray, 'My life, my work', pt 4

37: 'had some echoes' Interview with Andrew Robinson

37: 'daring and profound revelation' Ray, 'Thoughts on film-making', unfinished article in shooting notebook for *Aparajito* written after the film's Calcutta release in 1956

37: 'For some time after Sarbajaya's death' Quoted in *Eksan*, Calcutta, autumn 1984: 330

37: 'of improvisations on that' Ray, 'Thoughts on film-making', unfinished article in shooting notebook for *Aparajito* written after the film's Calcutta release in 1956

38: 'very touched by the fact' Interview with Andrew Robinson

38: 'Lila was his childhood companion' Banerji, *Aparajito*: 226

38: 'They have nice conversations' Interview with Andrew Robinson
39: '*March 4* [1956] – Visited the Durga Temple' Ray, *Our Films Their Films*: 27
40: 'Why did the unknown hold' Banerji, *Aparajito*: 33
41: 'because any direct statement' Interview with Andrew Robinson
42: 'A western viewer ignorant of' Ray, 'Under western eyes': 272
42: 'Very well, just tell me' Banerji, *Aparajito*: 196
42: 'Harihar Ray was a Brahmin' Banerji, *Pather Panchali*: 23

Chapter 3 An Epic in Production: Making the Apu Trilogy

45: 'Who would come to see an old hag' Ray, *My Years with Apu*: 58
45: 'They were stupid people' Interview with Andrew Robinson
46: 'It looks as if I'll have to rot' Letter to Norman Clare, 22 May 1948
46: 'in the dim light of a mango grove' Ray, 'My life, my work', pt 4
46: 'nasty old man' Interview with Andrew Robinson
47: 'The moment you are on the set' *Our Films Their Films*: 34
47: 'Little did I know then' Ibid.: 51
47: 'He looked so right' Interview with Bert Cardullo, in Cardullo (ed.): 182
48: 'safer with non-actors' Interview with James Blue, *Film Comment*, New York, summer 1968: 10
48: 'The first remark Manikda made' Das Gupta interview in Krupanidhi and Srivastava (eds), *Montage*: unpaginated
49: 'most outstanding performance' Ray, *My Years with Apu*: 57
49: 'I was a nobody at that time' Interview with Andrew Robinson
51: '[When] I cast my mind back' Ray, *My Years with Apu*: 54
51: 'But what part can I play at the age of 80?' Ibid.: 48

51: 'She was constantly aware' Ray, *Bisay Chalachchitra*: 103
52: 'I think this feat brought me' Ray, *My Years with Apu*: 66
52: 'Satyajit seemed a different person' Subrata Banerji, *Film World*, Bombay, April–May 1971: 34
53: 'The film people are 'ere …good this year.' Ray, *Bisay Chalachchitra*: 104–05
56: 'Mercifully, there were no jurors' Ray, 'Our festivals, their festivals'
56: '10 a.m.–12 noon' Mrinal Sen, *Views on Cinema*, Calcutta: Ishan, 1977: 4
56: 'and wondered each time' Ray, *Our Films Their Films*: 180
56: 'landmark' Message of appreciation of Bimal Roy on the occasion of a retrospective screening of Roy's films, Calcutta, Nov. 1986
57: 'completely apathetic' Letter to Marie Seton, 28 Nov. 1955
57: 'The rushes told us that' Interview with Andrew Robinson
58: 'their power and atmosphere' Ibid.
58: 'He felt it was very high quality' Ibid.
58: 'Do you think you could let us have this film' Ray, 'Under western eyes': 269
59: 'Can't you inject a message' Quoted in Ray, *My Years with Apu*: 60
59: 'My impression is that even when exploited' Quoted in Seton: 96
60: 'They get the money but' Quoted in Seton: 96
60: 'It was very unpleasant ... which we didn't know at the time.' Interview with Andrew Robinson
64: 'Today we will carry you out' Ray, *Bisay Chalachchitra*: 103
64: 'Don't be afraid to distort your face' Interview with Andrew Robinson
64: 'special, heightened quality' Interview with Dhritiman Chatterji, *Cinema Vision India*, 1:4 (1980): 15
65: 'Within seconds, the camera was set up' Quoted in Firoze Rangoonwalla, *Satyajit Ray's Art*, New Delhi: Clarion, 1980: 125

67: 'Suddenly I noticed this phenomenon' Interview with Andrew Robinson

67: 'a fine, sincere piece of film-making' Quoted in Ray, 'Under western eyes': 269

67: 'I recognised the footage' Letter to Andrew Robinson, 19 June 1987

68: 'a most remarkable film' Letter, 20 Nov. 1954, quoted in Chandak Sengoopta, '"The universal film for all of us, everywhere in the world": Satyajit Ray's *Pather Panchali* (1955) and the shadow of Robert Flaherty', *Historical Journal of Film, Radio and Television*, 29 (2009): 290

68: 'sort of hummed' Interview with Andrew Robinson

68: 'certainly a stroke of inspiration' Foreword to Ray, *The Apu Trilogy*: v

68: 'Now let's do a piece for such and such' Interview with Dhritiman Chatterji, *Cinema Vision India*, 1:4 (1980): 14

68: 'hectic … with Ravi Shankar' Ray's sleeve-note for Ravi Shankar, *Music from Satyajit Ray's Apu Trilogy*, EMI (India), 1978 (LP recording)

69: 'When we started recording, I kept signalling' Interview with Dhritiman Chatterji, *Cinema Vision India*, 1:4 (1980): 15

69: 'The effort to catch' Ray, 'Under western eyes': 269

69: 'What turned out to be a real nightmare' Ray, *My Years with Apu*: 79–80

70: 'It was then that I realised' Quoted in Chandak Sengoopta, 'Park Av. Panchali', *Outlook*, New Delhi, 8 Dec. 2008: 71

71: 'The audience was more interested' Chidananda Dasgupta, *The Cinema of Satyajit Ray*, 2nd edn, New Delhi: National Book Trust, 2001: 41

71: 'extremely discouraged … rapt attention.' Interview with Andrew Robinson

72: 'All middle-aged and older men' R. P. Gupta, *Sunday*, Calcutta, 5–11 Jan. 1986

72: 'I am on the verge of a new venture' Letter to Gerson da Cunha, Feb. 1956, in Krupanidhi and Srivastava (eds), *Montage*: unpaginated

73: 'smooth, page-turning professionalism' Arlene Croce, 'Pather Panchali and Aparajito', *Film Culture*, New York, 19 (1959): 48

73: 'That is a very shrewd comment' Interview with Andrew Robinson

73: 'It is always a problem with this kind of film … after a certain point' Ibid.

74: 'I was absolutely overwhelmed' Banerji interview in Krupanidhi and Srivastava (eds), *Montage*: unpaginated

74: '*1 March 1956* – Set out at 5 a.m.' Ray, *Our Films Their Films*: 25–26

75: 'Besides its truthful character' Mitra interview in Krupanidhi and Srivastava (eds), *Montage*: unpaginated

78: 'We were to a great extent Apus of our time' Interview with Andrew Robinson

78: 'We made her wear a sari' Interview with Andrew Robinson

78: 'Manikda is a tremendous actor' Interview with Andrew Robinson

78: 'I thought I could hardly expect him' Ray, *My Years with Apu*: 132

79: 'As soon as I decided to do *Aparajito*' Interview with Andrew Robinson

79: 'The river was just right' Ray, *My Years with Apu*: 136

80: 'The scene was going well' Ibid.: 142–43

Chapter 4 Working with Ravi Shankar: The Music of the Apu Trilogy

83: 'In the last couple of days' Shankar's sleeve-note for his *Farewell, My Friend…*, HMV (India), 1992 (audio-cassette recording)

84: 'He made such sublime films' Shankar: 125
84: 'the best film he made' Ibid.: 124–25
84: 'Ray understood Indian classical music' Interview with Ranjan Dasgupta, *Times of India*, 16 March 2009
84: 'Here was a director' Interview with Ranjan Dasgupta, *The Hindu*, 20 Feb. 2009
84: 'We became known to each other' Shankar: 121
85: 'One of the first things that Ravi Shankar ... over three days.' Ray's sleeve-note for Ravi Shankar, *Music from Satyajit Ray's Apu Trilogy*, EMI (India), 1978 (LP recording)
87: 'There is one scene in *Apur Sansar*' Foreword to Ray, *The Apu Trilogy*: vi
88: 'This caused a problem for Ravi Shankar' Ray, *My Years with Apu*: 78
88: 'In *Aparajito*, after Harihar's death' Interview with Cardullo, in Cardullo (ed.): 188
88: 'This was true – it was a hit-and-run affair' Shankar: 125
89: 'He is competent' Shankar interview in Krupanidhi and Srivastava (eds), *Montage*: unpaginated
89: 'We had a slight misunderstanding' Shankar: 125
89: 'The average middle-class Bengali' Interview with Dhritiman Chatterji, *Cinema Vision India*, 1:4 (1980): 18
89: 'but the challenge' Ray, *Bisay Chalachchitra*: 67

Chapter 5 *Pather Panchali*: Critique

91: 'I can never forget the excitement' *Eksan*, Calcutta, autumn 1987: 226 (translation of remarks made in Moscow in 1975, authenticated by Kurosawa in a letter to Andrew Robinson in 1988)
91: 'The best technique is the one' Interview with Andrew Robinson
92: 'In the West, we are conditioned' Wood: 7–8
92: 'Where poetry is coextensive' Sukumar Ray, 'The spirit of Rabindranath Tagore', *Quest*, London, Oct. 1913: 56–57

93: 'the very slow introductory movement' Shankar: 318
100: 'Not to have seen the cinema of Ray' *Eksan*, Calcutta, autumn 1987: 226 (translation of remarks made in Moscow in 1975, authenticated by Kurosawa in a letter to Andrew Robinson in 1988)
105: 'lost in thought' Banerji, *Pather Panchali*: 297
107: 'It's very complicated' Interview with Andrew Robinson
107: 'I have a feeling that the really crucial moments' Ibid.

Chapter 6 *Aparajito*: Critique

109: 'In *Aparajito*, Ray's unorthodox approach' Mrinal Sen, 'The time of the prologue is eternity', *Sunday Statesman*, Calcutta, 6 Nov. 1983
111: 'A train rumbles across a bridge' Ray, *The Apu Trilogy*: 61
115: 'A small action – which speaks volumes' Chakraborty: 290
116: 'a dewdrop that reflects' Interview with Folke Isaksson, *Sight and Sound*, London, summer 1970: 120
117: 'It is a nucleus' E. M. Forster, 'Pan', *Abinger Harvest*, London: Edward Arnold, 1936: 311
117: 'a spontaneous burst of applause' Ray, 'Our festivals, their festivals'
120: 'I hate conventional time lapses' Interview with Hugh Grey, *Film Quarterly*, Berkeley, winter 1958: 7
124: 'Goodness knows how many films' Ray, 'My life, my work', pt 4

Chapter 7 *The World of Apu*: Critique

127: 'What happens to Apu now?' Quoted in Ray, *My Years with Apu*: 119
128: 'surely one of the most moving films' Wood: 61
135: 'one of the cinema's classic affirmative depictions' Ibid.: 72
138: 'The fact of the death of the wife' Interview with Andrew Robinson

140: 'Being alone in these isolated places' Banerji, *Aparajito*: 316

Chapter 8 From Calcutta to Cannes: The Reception of the Apu Trilogy

148: 'My emotions after seeing' Bidyut Sarkar, *The World of Satyajit Ray*, 2nd edn, New Delhi: UBSPD, 1993: 15
148: 'preferably by myself' Quoted in Bidyut Sarkar, *The World of Satyajit Ray*, 2nd edn, New Delhi: UBSPD, 1993: 15
148: 'I think Ed' Letter to Marie Seton, 5 Nov. 1967
150: 'The festival finished with a week' Lindsay Anderson, *Observer*, London, 13 May 1956
150: 'Here is the discovery' Lotte Eisner, 'Cannes Film Festival 1956', *Salt Lake Post*, Calcutta, 25 Aug. 2007: 33 (special issue on *Pather Panchali*)
151: 'The initial reaction was' Interview with Andrew Robinson
151: 'squirming… "Leone d'Oro".' Ray, 'Our festivals, their festivals'
152: 'But now I hope Ray will' Penelope Houston: interview with Andrew Robinson
152: 'Now that I look back' Dilys Powell, *Sunday Times*, 13 May 1956
152: 'at a second look' Ibid., 22 Dec. 1957
153: 'I watched the audience surge' Ray, 'Under western eyes': 271
154: 'The entire conventional approach' Quoted in Seton: 165
154: 'The Indian film, *Pather Panchali*' Bosley Crowther, *New York Times*, 23 Sept. 1958
156: 'This is a picture of India' Ibid., 28 Sept. 1958
156: 'irresistible human appeal' Ray, 'The new cinema and I', *Cinema Vision India*, 1:3 (1980): 15
156: 'perhaps the finest piece' *Time*, 20 Oct. 1958
156: 'a demonstration of what a man' John McCarten, *New Yorker*, 1 Nov. 1958

156: 'I don't know anyone who' Arlene Croce, 'Pather Panchali and Aparajito', *Film Culture*, New York, 19 (1959): 46, 50

156: 'reviewer after reviewer … illusion' Chandak Sengoopta, '"The universal film for all of us, everywhere in the world": Satyajit Ray's *Pather Panchali* (1955) and the shadow of Robert Flaherty', *Historical Journal of Film, Radio and Television*, 29 (2009): 278, 285

157: 'he is still a poet' Arlene Croce, 'The World of Apu', *Film Culture*, New York, 21 (1960): 64

157: 'The connoisseur must feel' Paul Beckley, *New York Herald Tribune*, 5 Oct. 1960

157: 'One of the great cinematic experiences' Contribution by Martin Scorsese on the occasion of Ray's 70th birthday in Nemai Ghosh, *Satyajit Ray at 70*, Brussels: Eiffel Editions, 1991: 116–17

158: 'You won a prize at Cannes?' Quoted in Ray, *Our Films Their Films*: 139

158: 'absolutely terrified by … as it has ever been.' Letter to Lester James Peries, 7 Dec. 1958

Chapter 9 Apu in the East and West: The Trilogy and Ray Today

161: 'I must admit I get rather restive' Contribution by Arthur C. Clarke on the occasion of Ray's 70th birthday in Nemai Ghosh, *Satyajit Ray at 70*, Brussels: Eiffel Editions, 1991: 90

161: 'There's no question that *Pather Panchali*' Interview with Andrew Robinson

162: 'What does Ray portray in the Apu Trilogy' *Probe India*, Oct. 1980

164: 'this holy cow' Ibid.

164: 'The Modern India you speak of' Ibid.

164: 'a very dangerous, very vicious' Interview with Andrew Robinson

165: 'In a way, they mirror the fact' *Times of India*, 4 May 2009

166: '"I can never forget the excitement"' 'Satyajit Ray' in Salman Rushdie, *Imaginary Homelands: Essays and Criticism 1981–1991*, London: Granta, 1991: 107
167: 'Satyajit Ray's Apu Trilogy follows' James Christopher, *The Times*, 25 Aug. 2005
168: 'This first film by the masterly Satyajit Ray' Pauline Kael, *New Yorker*, 29 Aug. 2005
169: 'But why should the West care?' Ray, *Our Films Their Films*: 161
169: 'The cultural gap' Interview with Andrew Robinson
169: 'It is better not to spend too much' Ibid.
170: 'someone who sets himself' Interview with Andrew Robinson
170: 'found himself temperamentally unsuited' Letter to Marie Seton, 12 May 1978
171: 'No! With you it'll be different' Interview with Wendy Allen and Roger Spikes, *Stills*, London, autumn 1981: 46
171: 'I always regard Ray' Interview, *India Today*, 15 Feb. 1983
172: 'only a name' Interview with Andrew Robinson
172: 'Olympian heights' Letter to Saeed Jaffrey, 28 Aug. 1976
172: 'with a Satyajit Ray mind' Guha Thakurta interview in Krupanidhi and Srivastava (eds), *Montage*: unpaginated
172: 'Popular taste … Western' Ray interview in Krupanidhi and Srivastava (eds), *Montage*: unpaginated
172: 'I do not know of a single film-maker' Ray, *Our Films Their Films*: 98
173: 'tame, torpid versions … spoon-feeding' Ray, 'Under western eyes': 269
173: 'You'll find directors here' Interview with Udayan Gupta, *Cineaste*, New York, 12:1 (1982): 29
173: 'No matter how you make your film' 'Convocation Address' in Swapan Majumdar (ed), *Satyajit Ray Retrospective Souvenir: The Second Decade*, Calcutta, 1979: 6
173: 'which, in films, means anybody' Ray, *Our Films Their Films*: 12

173: 'what passed for criticism' Ray, 'Under western eyes': 269

174: 'What is attempted in most of my films' Ibid.: 274

174: 'I am sure Chaplin's name' Preface dated 4 April 1989 to *Charles Chaplin: A Centenary Tribute*, Calcutta, 1989 (brochure)

175: 'They are not, like the Americans' Contribution by V. S. Naipaul on the occasion of Ray's 70th birthday in Nemai Ghosh, *Satyajit Ray at 70*, Brussels: Eiffel Editions, 1991: 109

175: 'Like all Ray's late films' Nigel Andrews, *Financial Times*, 18 Nov. 1993

Select Bibliography

This is a highly selective bibliography, restricted mainly to works referred to in the text. For a fuller bibliography, see my two books: *Satyajit Ray: The Inner Eye*, especially the first edition (London: Andre Deutsch, 1989), and *Satyajit Ray: A Vision of Cinema*. Interviews with Ray are not included; they appear in the References.

Books by Satyajit Ray

The Apu Trilogy, Calcutta: Seagull, 1985 (English version by Shampa Banerji of the screenplay based on the original films in Bengali, with a foreword by Satyajit Ray)

Bisay Chalachchitra (On Cinema), 2nd edn, Calcutta: Ananda, 1982 (articles in Bengali, translated as *Speaking of Films*, New Delhi: Penguin, 2005)

Jakhan Chhoto Chhilam (When I Was Small), Calcutta: Ananda, 1982 (memoirs of childhood, translated as *Childhood Days*, New Delhi: Penguin, 1998)

My Years with Apu, London: Faber & Faber, 1997 (memoirs)

Our Films Their Films, New Delhi: Orient Longman, 1976 (articles in English)

Articles by Satyajit Ray

'My life, my work', *Telegraph*, Calcutta, 27 Sept.–1 Oct. 1982, in five parts (Amal Bhattacharji lecture delivered on 21

Sept.), republished in Tarapada Banerji, *Satyajit Ray: A Portrait in Black and White*, New Delhi: Penguin, 1993: 15–28

'Our festivals, their festivals', *Statesman*, Calcutta, 3–17 Jan. 1982 (supplement on the occasion of Filmotsav 82, international film festival in Calcutta)

'Under western eyes', *Sight and Sound*, London, autumn 1982: 269–74 (article on western attitudes to Indian cinema)

Books by Others

Banerji, Bibhutibhusan, *Pather Panchali: Song of the Road*, (T. W. Clark and Tarapada Mukherji, trans), London: George Allen & Unwin, 1968

Banerji, Bibhutibhusan, *Aparajito (The Unvanquished)*, (Gopa Majumdar, trans.), New Delhi: HarperCollins, 1999

Cardullo, Bert, ed., *Satyajit Ray: Interviews*, Jackson: University Press of Mississippi, 2007

Chakraborty, Ujjal, *The Director's Mind: A Step by Step Study of the Process of Film-making*, New Delhi: Alchemy, 2008

Das, Santi, ed., *Satyajit Ray: An Intimate Master*, New Delhi: Allied Publishers, 1998 (collected reviews and articles on Ray's films)

Krupanidhi, Uma and Anil Srivastava, eds, *Montage*, Bombay: Anandam Film Society, July 1966 (special issue on Satyajit Ray including reviews, articles on aspects of Ray, interviews with Ray, Bansi Chandragupta, Subrata Mitra, Ravi Shankar and Ray's actors; the screenplay of *Nayak* in English; and two pieces by Ray – 'Some aspects of my craft' and the commentary of B. D. Garga's documentary film about Ray)

Robinson, Andrew, *Satyajit Ray: The Inner Eye*, 2nd edn, London: I.B.Tauris, 2004

Robinson, Andrew, (with photographs by Nemai Ghosh), *Satyajit Ray: A Vision of Cinema*, London: I.B.Tauris, 2005

Seton, Marie, *Satyajit Ray: Portrait of a Director*, extended edn, London: Dennis Dobson, 1978

Shankar, Ravi, *Raga Mala: The Autobiography of Ravi Shankar*, Guildford: Genesis Publications, 1997

Wood, Robin, *The Apu Trilogy*, London: Studio Vista, 1972

Index